Personal Motivation

A Model for Decision Making

Robert P. Cavalier

Westport, Connecticut
London

Library of Congress Cataloging-in-Publication Data

Cavalier, Robert P., 1933–
    Personal motivation : a model for decision making / Robert P.
Cavalier.
      p.   cm.
    Includes bibliographical references and index.
    ISBN 0–275–96168–0 (alk. paper)
    1. Motivation (Psychology) 2. Decision making. I. Title.
    BF503.C39   2000
    153.8—dc21   99–34426

British Library Cataloguing in Publication Data is available.

Library of Congress Catalog Card Number: 99–34426
ISBN: 0–275–96168–0

First published in 2000

Praeger Publishers, 88 Post Road West, Westport, CT 06881
An imprint of Greenwood Publishing Group, Inc.
www.praeger.com

Printed in the United States of America

The paper used in this book complies with the
Permanent Paper Standard issued by the National
Information Standards Organization (Z39.48–1984).

10 9 8 7 6 5 4 3 2 1

Copyright Acknowledgment

The author and publisher gratefully acknowledge permission for use of the following material:

Excerpts from *Explaining Hitler* by Ron Rosenbaum. Copyright © 1998 by Ron Rosenbaum.
Reprinted by permission of Random House, Inc. and Macmillan.

To Caryl,

where life begins

Contents

Preface

When we were kids, my brother and I waited up for my father to come home a little after eight o'clock each night so we could have dinner together. Although most children our age were already in bed, Al and I stayed up to greet our father and to sit at the kitchen table with him. My father had just finished thirteen hours at his job, and I guess having dinner with his two boys was part of his reward for such a hard day's work. Dinner steaming on the stove was also part of the reward. My mother's look, her voice, and kiss were, of course, a big part.

There was always talking, and dinner was enjoyable most times, even if it did not consist of much more than string beans and boiled potatoes in tomato sauce left over from Sunday's spaghetti. Sometimes Al and I would complain when we asked, "What's for dinner?" and my mother's reply was, "Grazia di Dio"—"The grace of God." It was not much to look at or eat, but it was filling if you could handle it.

But my father never complained about dinner, or about how hard he worked, or about how tired he was. He pushed on from day to day and from year to year with love in his heart and dedication in every motion of his mind and body. He was completely committed to his family and lived out his conviction to his death at the early age of forty-eight. My father's name was Alfred, but everyone called him Fritz. Fritz was taken out of school in the third grade and never saw another classroom. He was put to work in his father's barbershop, where he cleaned spittoons and polished mirrors. He was made to wear long pants instead of knickers (I even wore knickers to school) so he would appear older, and at the age of ten, was assigned his own barber chair. He worked at his chair with his brother, Bob, at his side for thirty-five years, six days a week without a vacation. Unless Christmas fell on a Monday or a Saturday he never had two days off in a row. In a typical week he worked eighty hours since Saturday hours were 7:00 A.M. to 10:00 P.M. (a very late supper on Saturdays).

I mention this specifically because I probably will have no better opportunity to honor my father and mother, their courage, and the love they gave each other for strength. But I would add also that in a very real way, this book began at my kitchen table where I had dinner with my parents and where, later, my mother would pour coffee as I studied into the late hours.

Fritz is the guiding model for this book, which is about personal motivation and living by convictions and dedication to a purpose beyond our own self-interests. Fritz never met my wife, Caryl, but she has also been a guiding model, because like Fritz, she is also completely committed to her family, where her heart resides and her spirit is replenished, although it is not always easy going.

Commitment is almost always not easy, which means that a committed life is not an easy life, but, although difficult, it is inherently rewarding. Fritz taught me that a rewarding life is living through and with one's commitments, even if it meant, in his case, dying a young man. He has also shown me that a psychology aimed at human happiness is a false psychology unless it is tied to effort. Our greatest psychologists knew this. Sigmund Freud knew this, William James knew this, and my spiritual mentor for this book, Gordon Allport, knew this very well.

And so I went to the task of writing—never knowing if and when the book would ever get done, or for that matter, what final form it would take. I commend it to you nervously and with hesitation. I guess everyone would agree that writing is that special kind of human activity that is always difficult to do well, so this self-inflicted task has been, for me, a bumpy road at best.

Throughout the book I refer to a text that I have used in three editions since I began to teach History and Systems of Psychology. The text, *An Introduction to the History of Psychology*, by B. R. Hergenhahn, is one from which I have learned a great deal—not only the historical facts of psychology, but also unwritten things such as the connectedness of ideas and themes, and the spirit of the times as Professor Hergenhahn moves the reader from one generation of thinkers to the next. I also have observed, how successfully I'm not sure, what good book writing is all about.

Professor Hergenhahn develops his points, from chapter to chapter, by carefully choosing ideas and quotations from hundreds of original sources. He has provided a quotation from the learning theorist Edward Chace Tolman that fits nicely my own experience in writing this book:

[My theory] may well not stand up to any final canons of scientific procedure. But I do not much care. I have liked to think about psychology in ways that have proved congenial to me. Since all the sciences, and especially psychology, are still immersed in such tremendous realms of the uncertain and the unknown, the best that any individual scientist, especially any psychologist, can do seems to be to follow his own gleam and his own bent, however inadequate they may be. In fact, I suppose that actually this is what we all do. In the end, the only sure criterion is to have fun. And I have had fun.[1]

NOTE

1. Edward Chace Tolman, *Principles of Purposive Behavior* in *Psychology: A Study of Science*, vol. 2 (New York: McGraw Hill, 1959) 92–157, in B. R. Hergenhahn, *An Introduction to the History of Psychology* (Pacific Grove, Calif.: Brooks/Cole Publishing Co., 1997), 379.

Acknowledgments

Many people have influenced this effort, some of the heart and some of the mind. Heart comes first, because that's where the energy and commitment reside—that's what propelled this effort forward. My wife, Caryl, who has captured my heart, has breathed life into this project right from the start. Without her love and belief in me, this never would have happened. Our children also, Bob, Bill, and Molly, were most interested and supportive and always were excited to watch pages pile up on the dining room table. I have always been inspired by their kindness and love for family.

I have mentioned my parents, who caused me to take the path I took because they were convinced I had the stuff to achieve, even to excel. My older brother, Al, my only sibling, was always part of the rooting section. He even helped pay my tuition after our father died. Like Al, my lifelong friend Gus Jentile has shown me the way in many ways. Gus's capacity to love and to understand are a permanent part of my experience.

Of the mind there are many great teachers I have had from grade school days through my years at Columbia. I remember especially Sr. Marie Imelda (grade school), James C. G. Conniff (literature), Robert J. Roth, S. J. (philosophy), Allen R. Solem (psychology) and Robert Sessions Woodworth, who at age eighty-nine taught me the history of psychology. (I remember that he once apologized to the class for not being as prepared as he would have liked because he had spent the day reading galleys of his book *Dynamics of Behavior*, published that year.) I also want to mention, for sheer intellectual stimulation, James D. Wilson, who ran a seminar on *Huckleberry Finn* with ten faculty members at Quarry Farm, Mark Twain's summer residence now operated by Elmira College.

As the writing proceeded, many people pitched in to help, but I must especially mention Jani Hart, who remained loyal to this project from the outset and gave most graciously of her talent and her time as each page of each draft was crafted through several cycles and readied for reviewers and editors. Without Jani's dedication and encouragement, this project would still be in my desk drawer.

Thanks also to Kathleen Galvin, who repeatedly chased out books for me from libraries throughout the country. In short time, she located every one I needed. I am indebted also to the talent of Jan Kather for the design of those figures in the text. Chris Hummer provided assistance and encouragement in the early stages of this project. I will always be most appreciative of her help. I want to thank also President Thomas Meier and Dean Bryan Reddick, who expressed interest in this project from the beginning and who paved the way through release time and sabbatical leave.

Finally, after getting lost in the woods, there were the reviewers who guided me out. Their careful reading of an inadequate text pointed me in the right direction. Whatever value the book may have is due in major part to my reviewers and their better ideas. I want to thank B. R. Hergenhahn, whose prodigious scholarship revealed so many flaws in the manuscript and whose corrections and comments saved the book from the circular file.

Charles Mitchell and John Fratarcangelo brought needed light and balance to a work that was woefully obscure and out of balance. Their time and patience in reading and commenting on the text is much appreciated. Thanks also to Larry Schein, who graciously responded to my request and who significantly improved what I tried to say in Chapter Nine. Rafiuddin Ahmed and Diane Maluso also took on the tough assignment of reading and commenting on a manuscript so needing of repair. They stuck to the task and have helped me tremendously. Thank you all, reviewers, and thanks also to my editor, Nita Romer, at Greenwood Publishing Group. She believed in this project, saw something in it that I hope others see, and with the guiding talent of Megan Peckman, production editor, it was brought forward to completion.

Introduction

Although this book will be published as we end one century and begin another, it is not about endings or new beginnings. Books have been written about the end of history and the end of science. Indeed, Fred Newman and Lois Holzman have written a book they have titled *The End of Knowing*.[1] But this book is not about ending anything—certainly not in psychology, which has completed a century of incredibly fruitful production in psychological theory and applications. It has been the century of Sigmund Freud, Carl Jung, Edward Thorndike, John Watson, B. F. Skinner, Gordon Allport, Abraham Maslow, David McClelland, Douglas McGregor and so many other thinkers who have shaped our consciousness and helped us in our attempt to gain insight into our human condition.

We know that as a people we are embedded in a culture, which means that any attempt to answer the question, "Where is humanity now?" must take into account cultural factors such as education, technology, and dominant values. Any attempt, therefore, to place humanity into a future time is limited by shifting cultural forces. So what, then, has psychology accomplished if culture is of such overriding importance? Psychologists will answer this question differently, but my attempt at an answer is the reason for writing a book on *personal motivation* as related to the *self*. Psychology has preserved the self as a viable concept. It has theorized about self, it has written books about self, it has attempted to measure the self, it has assigned many powers to self, and it has constructed a whole new self vocabulary. Terms such as *self-concept*, *self-esteem*, *self-development*, and *self-actualization* are typical expressions that someday will be used with terms such as *psychoanalysis* and *behavior modification* (getting old already) to describe twentieth-century psychology. The paradox of twentieth-century psychology is although it has preserved the self as a viable concept, it also has devoted most of its intellectual resources to making psychology into an empirical science in which observation and measurement rule. This has included the measurement of the self, whereby a variety of personality tests, interest inventories, and self-assessment instruments have been developed based on an assumed normal distribution of human characteristics. There are also some non-normative measures such as the Rorschach Test, which most hard-nosed empiricists see as more mystical than real.

All of this being the case, personality and interest tests have never really come close to defining the self, but at best may describe how the self might function in a given situation. It's called *operationism*, which is a way of avoiding essential definitions. In fact, empirical psychology has survived all these years by operationalizing psychological concepts. (The concept, therefore, becomes defined by how it is measured.) Little wonder that the self has eluded definition. Yet it has endured as a concept despite the empirical onslaught of twentieth-century psychology, which I have recently heard referred to as "the cult of empiricism."

This book is yet another book about the self coming at a time when post-modern psychology sees the self as largely diminished, in jeopardy, without personal capacity and meaning, and resulting in wanton, reckless, and often hostile activity.[2] In my view, what has diminished is not the self per se but the capacity within the self to exercise its own force of will. Will and self coexist as a unity within the person, and it is this unity, culture notwithstanding, that constitutes what it means to be a human being. What we are experiencing today, which postmodernists describe as a loss of self, is better stated as a loss of will, personal commitment, and convictions. Belief systems and personal convictions have become blurred by a conglomeration of factors that make up our postmodern times. These include opportunism, expediency, mass marketing, and an impersonal technology that presents us each day with a dizzying array of choices. The person blinks and reacts, and true deciding and willing are increasingly less in the picture. Hence the title of my book, *Personal Motivation: A Model for Decision Making*.

In my writing, I have been influenced by the ideas of Gordon Allport, a "modernist" whose thoughts are my choice for a bridge to the next millennium. In my view, he has been psychology's best voice for the responsible individual whose motives are self-generated—where reaction to stimuli is less important than planning and forming ideals to live by. He has constructed the individual as a deliberating and responsible human being.

Allport has asked, "May not (sometimes at least) an acquired world-outlook constitute the central motive of life and, if it is disordered, the ultimate therapeutic problem? May not a person's philosophy of life, here and now, be a functionally autonomous motive? Need we always dig deeper than the present-ing phenomenology?"[3] I have tried in the pages that follow to pursue Allport's thesis. It is my attempt to deal with the question Allport proposes and to make those distinctions that he regards as important—distinctions based on a systems approach to understanding human motivation. Allport has used the term "person system."

Although I have come to this task from a humanistic–philosophical tradition, I know there would be no psychology today (and I probably wouldn't have my job) without the rigors of empirical investigation that have set psychology apart from philosophy and theology. I believe that empirical psychology must continue if we are not to submerge into the murky waters of phenomenology and romanticism. Psychology is a natural science—just a different kind of natural science. Kirk Schneider in his article, "Toward a Science of the Heart" has quoted William James:

When. . . we talk of "psychology as a natural science," we must not assume that that means a sort of psychology that stands at last on solid ground. It means just the reverse; it means a psychology particularly fragile, and into which the waters of metaphysical criticism leak at every point, a psychology whose elementary assumptions and data must be reconsidered in wider connections and translated into other terms. (William James, 1892/1961, pp. 334–335)[4]

In this sense we begin the twenty-first century as we began the twentieth, with a lot of good information in between.

NOTES

1.   Fred Newman and Lois Holzman, *The End of Knowing: A New Developmental Way of Learning* (New York: Routledge, 1997).

2.   A postmodern viewpoint sees the self as constantly under construction in a social arena of language and symbols. It is a view that holds that the person does not possess a unique self, but that the self is a continuing creation of social and cultural forces.

3.   Gordon W. Allport, "Comment on Earlier Chapters" in *Existential Psychology*, ed. Rollo May (New York: Random House, 1961), 98.

4.   William James, *Psychology: The Briefer Course* (New York: Harper Torchbooks, 1892/1961) in Kirk Schneider, "Toward a Science of the Heart," *American Psychologist* 53 (March 1998), 277.

CHAPTER 1

Thank You, Dr. Allport

Each person is an idiom. . . an apparent violation of the syntax of the species.

—Gordon W. Allport, *Becoming* (p. 19)

John Watson ranks among the most important psychologists of the twentieth century. He was the founder of the important movement in American psychology known as behaviorism and has had many followers, most notably the famous Harvard psychologist B. F. Skinner. Watson was a handsome, charming, and amazingly persuasive person who was able to get people to see things his way. He was also afraid of the dark.

As a young man, Watson persuaded the president of Furman University to accept him as a student at the age of fifteen despite his poor high school record. Later at the age of thirty-six, he was elected president of the American Psychological Association—only eleven years after completing his Ph.D. at the University of Chicago. He culminated his career in an occupation highly suited to his persuasive talents, earning $70,000 in 1930 as vice president of the J. Walter Thompson advertising agency. Watson was a forceful personality whose life reveals the American ethic of creating opportunity through personal initiative and performance. It is true, however, that he was also afraid of the dark and that as an adult when he felt depressed, he went to sleep with his light on. It is interesting, even disconcerting, that such a great talent could not rid himself of this troublesome behavior. And although it is interesting, it is of no great importance in our attempts to understand the man. He is understood best by his accomplishments and by their underlying motivations. The most we can know about the man are his motivated acts, which give his life its character and its meaning. To say that Watson was persuasive is useful; to say that he was afraid of the dark may be interesting, too, but those things really tell us little about the man as a motivated human being. They are personality characteristics, not motives.

With Watson, as with all of us, human beings are understood by their motivated acts. There is no better way. People with similar personality characteristics may be motivated in very different ways; conversely, people with very different personalities can be motivated in similar ways. It's one's motives that reveal the person to us.

Dan P. McAdams of Northwestern University devotes two chapters of his popular 1994 text *The Person* to motivational themes and the value of biographical analysis. He discusses the work of Henry A. Murray (to whom he dedicates the book) at the Harvard Psychological Clinic. In referring to Murray's idea of personology, McAdams says the following:

The directedness of human lives becomes apparent over time. A given momentary behavior may seem meaningless in light of the current situation in which it is embedded. But with respect to the person's life over time the behavior may be seen as a part of a *purposeful* [italics mine] sequence of actions. Time is the defining feature of the person.. .. While it is feasible to examine a person's life at a particular moment in time, one must never forget that such a venture represents an arbitrary selection of a part from the whole. One must never forget [Murray's dictum] that "the *history* of the organism *is* the organism."[1]

Later, McAdams describes the work of the philosopher Alasdair MacIntyre: "What is good for a single person is what contributes to the completion of his or her life story. What is good for humankind must be derived from an analysis of the features that are common to all life stories."[2]

It is for this reason that a solely empirical approach to human psychology is so limited, since it depreciates the role of human curiosity regarding our past as a people. Comparative psychology, which investigates the behavior of animals, is limited in what it can say about human beings since humans are neither rats nor pigeons. Like these animals, we behave, but to say that our motives can be understood by studying the behavior of rats or pigeons is nonsensical. Rats and pigeons do not have motives in the human sense of motivation. Moreover, one of the major tenets of humanistic psychology is that nothing substantive can be learned about human nature by studying the behavior of animals.

The philosopher Thomas Nagel wrote an article that has become a classic in his field.[3] The article carries the intriguing title *What Is It Like to Be a Bat?* In it, Nagel makes the point that there is "something it is like to be a bat," but that this "something" is out of the reach of human comprehension. He makes the convincing argument that although consciousness is a universal phenomenon, it is always a subjective reality. Whether Martian, human, or any other species, the subjective reality of the bat, rat, or wasp, its unique internal experience, is inaccessible to other conscious beings. A bat's conscious experience belongs forever and always to bats alone.

The article successfully divides reality into the objective and the subjective—that there *is* "something it is like to be a bat," that this "something" exists and is a part of reality, although it cannot be reduced to knowable parts in the objective order of things. It is subjectively whole and subjectively real.

And even though a person can never know what it is like to be a bat, we do know what it is like to be a human being. The "something it is like" to be human is shared by all humans—past, present, and to come. This experience is found in all human activities yet, paradoxically, it is one we are continually probing and is known perhaps best to the artist and the writer. We are constantly asking ourselves in our art and in our literature what is this "something" that it is like to be human. Personal motives and personal decisions certainly must be parts. Wondering, knowing, and creating are other important parts, but certainly our motives and our decisions are crucial elements in this human fabric—this human "something."

Motives are personal possessions; they have subjective reality. Motivated behavior is evaluative; it implies choice and decision. Evaluating and deciding are distinctly human acts. They belong to the *self*. An animal that has been conditioned to respond in certain ways is not evaluating nor deciding—not in the human sense. The animal is simply acting (or better, reacting) in ways that will provide reinforcement depending on previous reinforced activity. The animal may make a choice between alternative A or alternative B, but it is not a free choice if it has been conditioned by prior experience—and if it is a random choice, it is not really a choice at all. Animals may choose, but only humans decide. There is a great deal of difference. The psychologist Norman R. F. Maier, who has had considerable research background in both animal and human behavior, tells us that decision making is an integrating process that takes account of a multiplicity of variables including facts, values and feelings.[4] Human decision making is necessarily an evaluating and integrating process different in kind from the choice a rat in a Y maze makes in running down path A or B in its search for food. The best decisions are sponsored by human freedom; like motives, decisions are also personal possessions. Human nature, therefore, is best seen in terms of purpose and values rather than in terms of previously rewarded behavior. Henry Murray and Alasdair MacIntyre mentioned above would agree. Rats and pigeons do not deal with reality at this level; they are devoid of values and purposes. Humans have intentionality; animals do not. Indeed, we are evaluated more on our intentions than on our behavior. The person who shoots to kill and misses is certainly as much a killer as the person who hits the target. People are sinners or saints by virtue of motives, not behavior. The same behavior can be sponsored by very different motives. The obedient child may be obedient for a variety of reasons. It is the reasons behind the obedience, not the obedience per se, that tells us something about the child. A child who is obedient because he wants to ask his parents for a special privilege is very different from the child who is dutifully obedient to outshine his brother or sister. The motives are very different indeed.

To understand human behavior is very different from explaining behavior. The game of chess can be understood really only in terms of the personal strategies of the players (that "something it is like" to be a chess player). The analogy applies to human behavior. The movement of a rook can be explained by reference to the rules; however, it can be understood only by referring to the player. For this reason, it would be foolish to have two IBM computers play each other. It was the human component that made the playoffs between Gary Kasparov and the IBM computer of any value to observe. The difference is obvious and immense in its implication. For example, we can never understand humans by discovering rules of learning; by so doing, we can only explain how learning occurs. It is the behaviorist who attempts to understand human behavior in terms of rules—overlooking the person who is behaving. (Social-learning theory has fortunately inserted the person back into the behavioral paradigm, but a tenuous person, as we shall see.)

This book focuses squarely on the issue of human motives and values and their underlying dynamics. Much of psychology has been concerned with process, too little with content. To say, for example, that a person is high in "achievement motivation" tells us much less about the person than to say that the person is a Mafiosa chieftain or a corporation president.[5] Achievement motivation may be operative in both cases, but the content of the motives is really quite different. Many psychologists would deny the importance of such a distinction since achievement motivation supplies an explanation of motivation in both cases. Although psychologists may deny the importance of such a distinction, the distinction is still crucial.

Since humans can be adequately understood best in terms of their motivated acts, it becomes the first business of psychological science to investigate human motivation. It is the study of human motives that provides a fuller appreciation of humankind—in history, in the present, and for the future.

MOTIVATIONAL SYSTEMS

The great Harvard psychologist Gordon Allport spoke of systems theory in an address to the Personality and Social Psychology Division of the American Psychological Association on September 4, 1959.[6] (Apparently, a systems view of personality was very important to him since he also developed this idea in his book *Pattern and Growth in Personality*.[7]) In his talk, Allport distinguished among those personality theorists who subscribe to a quasi-closed system, those who propose an open system, and those who see personality as open to the environment but nonetheless "as something integumented, as residing within the skin"[8] This modified open system focuses on the internal dynamics of the individual and affirms that the person, although connected to the world, is nonetheless an integrated whole separate from the world. Postmodern theorists see the person as in flow with the fluctuating forces of change and that to understand the person is to understand all the forces impinging upon the person. Allport argues the "within-the-skin" view that, although the person is never static, the individual remains an integrated whole and can be thought of as distinct from the world. There are, of course, strong arguments on all sides of this issue, but this book attempts to present a modified open system viewpoint that holds that the person is both a unique self and an integration of interdependent motivational systems. To think of motivation as systems is extremely useful, and to think of the person as an integrated whole, as a unique self, is also useful. Allport says, "It is the duty of psychology, I think, to study the person-system, meaning thereby the attitudes, abilities, traits, trends, motives, and pathology of the individual—his cognitive styles, his sentiments, and individual moral nature and their interrelations."[9]

This book focuses on motives and proposes an interactive-systems approach to understanding human motivation. It proposes that there are three autonomous yet interdependent motivational systems that characterize all human conduct, and it is the study of these interdependent systems that provides a more adequate understanding of the workings of human nature. It is a *triarchic theory of motivation*.

SELF AS CENTRAL

A central notion in this theory of motivation is that the person is composed of a distinct self, contrary to prevalent postmodern thinking, that is reflected in, and perhaps even grows out of, the motivational process. Every person, alive, dead, or to be, owns a personal self, an ego, which is the object and subject of consciousness. Allport is emphatic on this point:

Without the coordinating concept of *person* (or some equivalent such as *self* or *ego*), it is impossible to account for the interaction of psychological processes. Memory affects perception, desire influences meaning, meaning determines action, and action shapes memory; and so on indefinitely. This constant interpenetration takes place within some boundary, and the boundary is the person.

The organization of thought or behavior can have no significance unless viewed as taking place within a definite framework. Psychological states do not organize themselves or lead independent existences. Their arrangement merely constitutes part of a larger arrangement—the personal life.

Such concepts as *function, adaptation, use* have no significance without reference to the person. If an adjustment takes place it must be an adjustment *of* something, *to* something, *for* something. Again the person is central.[10]

A second, equally important thesis is that the self is essentially autonomous and free to do and to be as the self so determines. The freedom to decide to be the kind of person one wishes is quintessential to human nature and forms a major tenet in the current theory. Without freedom, each person is completely determined by biological and environmental influences. Motivation exists within each one of us, and to some extent it is our freedom that justifies the use of such a term as motivation. This position is consistent with another major tenet of humanistic psychology—that one's personal reality is the primary guide for human behavior.

PERSON-SYSTEM

What is proposed is a shift in emphasis from theories of personality to a theory of motivation, taking the lead from Gordon Allport who suggested "the person-systems" as an approach to understanding human nature. This book will attempt to follow Allport's lead by proposing a *triarchic theory of motivation* as a "person system," which subsumes within it all we have learned about human personality. In this way, the various theories of personality can be integrated into a new theoretical structure.

The thesis, then, is that the self is composed of three autonomous motivational systems: the formative system, the operational system, and the thematic system. Each motivational system is autonomous, but there is a high degree of interdependence among them. The formative motivational system includes all developmental forces, which compel the individual to move in certain directions. This includes one's genetic makeup; learned behaviors, beliefs, and values; social norms and attitudes; and psychodynamic factors such as unconscious wishes, conflicts, and so on. The formative system is heavily loaded with feelings and propensities to see the world and behave in certain ways. It is dispositional. The operational system includes all current assessments and strategies in which there is a sense of evaluation, integration, choosing, and decision-making. Much of our lives' problem solving and choices are operational. The thematic system concerns one's values and purpose in living. The direction one takes in life is a function of the thematic system, which consists of three major motives that are both directional and futuristic, and which provide life with its worth and its meaning and grow out of our humanity and our freedom. Although certainly influenced by the other systems (they are interdependent) it is not determined by them; the autonomous self is the determining influence on the thematic motivational system.

The thematic system finds expression in three major motives:

1) Ego gratification

2) Self-actuation
3) Altruism

These three life motives may be viewed as fundamental themes that characterize so much of human existence. Some people possess these themes in varying degrees, whereas others' lives are dominated by one theme to the practical exclusion of the others. They are similar to Allport's reminder of "a bit of ancient Hindu wisdom, which says that we have four main desires: pleasure, success, "to do one's duty and discharge one's responsibility," and "to seek intensely for a grade of understanding—for a philosophical or religious meaning," which is a kind of desire discussed later in the book.[11]

Ego Gratification

This motive predominates in people who devote most of their conscious effort, time, and energy to activities that bring power, pleasure, or both. People characterized by such motives are always seeking ways to achieve power, status, wealth, and pleasure. For such people the purpose in living is to gratify one's ego by winning the adulation of others, by governing others' lives, by acquiring wealth and position, and by luxuries and pleasures. For such people power, praise, and pleasure provide the "kick" that makes life meaningful. Some individuals possess this motivation in the extreme, whereas for others it is less important or perhaps not significant at all. Few in our "achieving society" are without it completely. This is a complicated and treacherous motive, because power can become irresistible. Historical evidence abounds in support of the thesis that such people can be both corrupting and corruptible. It is also a motive that is not entirely compatible with the human condition, for as we shall see, the survival of the species depends not on power but on love. It should be stressed that not all people who achieve power are necessarily out for ego-gratification; sometimes power comes not by quest but by accomplishment, which is a totally different matter. However, to have great power and maintain humility and a sense of service to others can be an extremely difficult task, perhaps an impossible one. Traitors and conspirators we well know. Only extraordinary people can use power well and wisely. Perhaps they come to positions of leadership too infrequently.

The same may be said with respect to pleasure. The altruistic person who also enjoys sensual pleasures may do so fully and with relish. However, this does not mean that he lives a life directed to pleasure seeking. Indeed, those whose lives are not dedicated to pleasure frequently are free to savor pleasure more than the person who lives for pleasure's sake. The issue is not power or pleasure per se but the obsessive character of both in forming a theme for living. Alas, there are those whose whole lives are utterly given to power and pleasure and who never really achieve either. We know them as miserable people without joy and without hope. One cannot know joy or hope if one's life is given to power and pleasure in their various forms. Certainly there is no peace.

Self-Actuation

The term *self-actuation* is borrowed from other writers, notably Abraham Maslow, whose term *self-actualization* has meaning that is similar but somewhat different from this one.[12] Self-actuation means that motivation whereby individuals seek ways to fully express their interests, talents, and potentials as free human beings. Such people see life in terms of using their talents and expressing themselves creatively as people. Such people are typically unorthodox in their perceptions of life. They can be spirited or pensive, but inevitably, they experience an inner surge of growth and energy. They are vital people animated by their craft or their ideas. They find joy in doing, in creating, in performing, in experiencing themselves as people through their work and accomplishments.

For many, self-actuation is a major motivational theme in life. For others it is important but a subsidiary motive. There are many fortunate people whose careers develop out of this motivation. The concert pianist, the research scientist, and the professional athlete are all examples. Tiger Woods is regarded by many authorities as potentially the world's greatest golfer. His young age attests to the importance of self-actuation motivation, but the same may be true of the entrepreneur whose business is a way of expressing one's self creatively and innovatively as a person. Frequently, this theme is seen in many people who just enjoy doing, learning, and creating. It does not necessarily involve exceptional talent, but it always means using one's potential as a unique and growing human being.

It is interesting also that self-actuated people frequently have considerable influence and power over others simply by virtue of their knowledge and talent. Such would be true of the scholar or the artist, and although they may enjoy approbation and applause, they do not live their lives for approbation or applause. It is not the *first* purpose of their existence. The fact is that true scholarship or virtuosity can likely never be achieved with this sole end in view.

The following passage from Daniel Goleman's book *Emotional Intelligence* is instructive in this regard. In discussing what is called "flow," Goleman makes reference to the well received work of the University of Chicago psychologist Mihaly Csikszentmihalyi:

Because flow emerges in the zone in which activity challenges people to the fullest of their capacities, as their skills increase it takes heightened challenge to get into flow. . . . that the motivation to get better and better at something, be it playing the piano, dancing or gene-splicing is at least in part to stay in flow while doing it. Indeed in a study of two hundred artists eighteen years after they left art school, Csikszentmihalyi found that it was those who in their student days had savored the sheer joy of painting itself who had become serious painters. Those who had been motivated in art school by dreams of fame and wealth for the most part drifted away from art after graduating.[13]

Altruism

There are those people whose lives are directed to service. They see the first purpose of existence in terms of love of one's fellows. Such people generally live lives characterized by self-sacrifice for others. Ego gratification and self-actuation are not in themselves significant motivators for such people. For them, the time and energy of life is designed not to indulge one's self or express one's self but rather to surrender one's self to a just cause—that cause being the welfare of humankind.

Altruism in this sense is love—true love for one's fellows as frequently expressed in various forms of self-sacrifice. It is love, not in the sense of eros or erotic love, but rather in the sense of *caritas* or *agape*, which is love for humankind.[14]

Altruism forms the principal motivational theme for those people who seek opportunities to help other people. Sometimes this takes the form of great acts of sacrifice and heroism. More often, it is seen in the loving direction of a good parent, an understanding teacher, a compassionate counselor, or a good friend. (The Compeer organization, for example, recruits volunteers to spend time with someone receiving mental health therapy—to befriend someone who needs a friend.) The parent whose time and energy are dominated by a preoccupation for power, pleasure, or even creativeness can be less loving and giving as a parent than one who is motivated by a profound concern for one's family. Playing the role of parent, teacher, or counselor does not necessarily equate with true altruism. Sometimes, altruism is the most deceitful of all motives, because it can be replaced by egoistic concerns and the sense of self-importance associated with giving advice or teaching. These people are motivated not by altruism or self-actuation, but by ego gratification, which denies others the true opportunity to grow and to learn.

Before concluding this chapter, it is important to stress the fact that the thematic motivational system is rarely completely dominated by any one of the major thematic motives. For most of us, all three motives, in varying degrees, play a part in living. For some people, of course, the differences are often very significant and very noticeable to self and others. Consider Benito Mussolini, Amadeus Mozart, and Mother Teresa!

NOTES

1. Dan P. McAdams, *The Person: An Introduction to Personality Psychology* (New York, Harcourt Brace, 1994), 605.

2. Ibid., 748.

3. Thomas Nagel, "What Is It Like to Be a Bat?" in *Readings in Philosophy of Psychology*, vol. 1, ed. Ned Block (Cambridge, Mass.: Harvard University Press, 1980), 159–168.

4. Norman R. F. Maier, *Problem Solving and Creativity in Individuals and Groups* (Belmont, Calif.: Wadsworth, 1970).

Maier, who has worked and published extensively in problem solving and decision making, provides some excellent insights into the nature of human decision making. Maier has shown that there are two dimensions to human decisions: quality and acceptance. Quality refers to the importance or consequences inherent in a decision. Some decisions are just more important or consequential than others. Acceptance refers to the degree of human feeling surrounding the decision. Some decisions are marked by greater involvement and feeling than others—especially by people immediately affected by a decision. For Maier, an effective decision (ED) is a function of its quality times its acceptance; that is, $ED = Q \times A$.

Maier's analysis is useful in appreciating the elements involved in human decisions. Human decisions should take into account facts bearing upon decision quality as well as the perceptions and attitudes of people affected by the decision. This is a process of both evaluation and integration and is not reflected in the various choices animals make. Animal choices are influenced totally by prior experience. They do not attempt to anticipate human reactions and implications. For animals, choices are consummatory; for humans, decisions are precursors to future events. Humans make many choices, too, where quality and acceptance are not particularly relevant—which TV show to watch, for example—but these are not decisions in the best sense of the word. Again, animals choose but humans decide. There is a difference. (This topic is discussed more fully in Chapter Eight.)

5. Achievement motivation as a special form of learned motivation represented in certain societies has been identified and studied by David C. McClelland and his associates. They found that the motive to achieve was a learned motive with certain characteristics. They found, for example, that individuals high in achievement motivation or the need to achieve seek opportunities for challenge and competition and desire feedback on how well they are doing. They will take calculated risks to demonstrate to self and others how well they can perform, and like to know where they stand.

This research, conducted over several years in the fifties and sixties asked subjects to tell stories to ambiguous pictures found in the Thematic Apperception Test. (The TAT is discussed further in Chapter Four.) These "projections," as such stories are called, frequently revealed the individual's need to compete, succeed, or excel. This McClelland termed the *achievement motive*.

6. Gordon W. Allport, "The Open System in Personality Theory" *Journal of Abnormal and Social Psychology* 61 (1960), 301–310.

7. Gordon W. Allport, *Pattern and Growth in Personality* (New York: Holt, Rinehart and Winston, 1961), 567–571.

8. Allport, "The Open System in Personality Theory," 306.

9. Ibid., 306.

10. Allport, *Pattern and Growth in Personality*, 553.

11. Allport, "The Open System in Personality Theory," 304.

12. Abraham H. Maslow, "A Theory of Human Motivation," *Psychological Review* 50 (1943), 370–396.

Abraham Maslow is credited with the full development of the concept used by many other writers with varying degrees of emphasis. Maslow posed a hierarchy of human needs in which self-actualization represents the highest form or motivation which, when gratified, is the fullest expression of one's self. For Maslow, to be self-actualized is the human being's ultimate realization, a level that is achieved by regrettably few people.

13. Daniel Goleman, *Emotional Intelligence* (New York: Bantam Books, 1995), 93.

In his best-selling book *Emotional Intelligence*, Daniel Goleman discusses the connections between emotional responsiveness and personal adjustment issues. In his discussion of flow, he refers to Mihaly Csikszentmihalyi's 1990 book *Flow: The Psychology of Optimal Experience* (New York: Harper & Row, 1990) as well as personal interviews with him for *Newsweek* and *The New York Times*.

14. Rollo May indicates that there are four kinds of love in Western tradition—sex, eros, philia, and agape or caritas. Sex he describes as lust or libido, eros as the human need or drive to procreate the species, philia as friendship or brotherly love, and agape as man's devotion to the welfare of others. For a fascinating and prolonged discussion of this topic, the reader should see May's book, *Love and Will* (New York: Dell, 1969).

CHAPTER 2

Self and Will

> Psychology's new concern with values is at bottom a concern with choices, and therefore revives the problem of freedom.
>
> —Gordon W. Allport, *Becoming* (p. 83).

Some people found the film *The Truman Show* unsettling in the manner in which it allowed viewers to interpret reality. Like Thomas Nagel's "Bat," *The Truman Show* nicely illustrates the difference between subjective and objective forms of reality. Truman Burbank, unwittingly, has been the star of a TV show his whole life of thirty years until, in the closing scenes, he decides to move from TV reality to true reality. The audience has to deal with at least four realities: their own subjective realities as viewers, the objective reality of the movie, which can be discussed with other viewers, the objective reality of the TV show as it is staged and executed by the various TV players, and the subjective reality of Truman himself, who believes he is in the real world, which the audience knows to be fake.

Time magazine's review of the film had this to say:

The standard film. . . takes its audience on a familiar ride. Actors pretend to be heroes or villains doing amazing or funny things. And we, in an implied compact with the film-makers, pretend it's real. In *The Truman Show* the rules are more complicated. We are watching a movie that purports to be a TV show and that we (along with everyone else but Truman) know is fake. Occasionally, we watch "viewers" of the show, in their home or a bar, reacting to some dramatic moment. And at times we watch Christof [TV director] and his crew directing the show. Weir [movie director], like his alter ego Christof, lays the process of magicmaking and manipulation open before us. Here's how we do it, people: music and mirrors.[1]

Like the experience of seeing the movie, much of psychological theorizing is confusing because it is about different realities. There are the objective scientists (e.g., B. F. Skinner) who become the subjective interpreters and purveyors of ideas about a part of reality they have arbitrarily framed within their scientific studies, choosing to discount completely the subjective realities of the animals or people in their experiments. Some psychologists are far more concerned with the subjective realities of the people they study, but still insist on being objective scientists who are seeking and then interpreting people's subjective experiences (e.g., Sigmund Freud). This can get very messy and obscure. Others, trying to correct these problems, sit on both sides of the fence while claiming to be objective investigators. They have tried to design plausible paradigms (e.g., Albert Bandura) in which they include the person as part of a scientific formulation.

There are yet others, the so-called humanistic–existential psychologists, who, while rejecting scientific reductionism, claim to be objectively in search of the whole person. These people (e.g., Abraham Maslow) have found it necessary to wear a scientific mantle when all they really care about in their work is the subjective experience (the selves) of the people they study. Also, all of their theorizing is loaded with their own personal convictions and values.

All psychologists, myself included (I'm probably more humanistic than anything else) are intellectually disposed to one or more of these viewpoints. Let's look at them more carefully.

IDEAS AND REALITIES

The Freudian tradition holds that we are essentially determined by the events and conditions of our upbringing, and that the chief culprit for our failure to understand ourselves and achieve happiness is the id and the repressed content of the unconscious mind. Human motives, according to Freud, are unknown even to the self since they exist in the dynamic urgings of the unconscious. According to strict psychoanalytic theory, each person is essentially at the mercy of all those anxiety-producing experiences in life that have been converted into unconscious material—material that is constantly seeking expression and does escape from time to time in such symbolic transformations as neurotic symptoms, dreams, and slips of the tongue (the so-called Freudian slips.) and other mistakes people may make.[2]

It is basically a negative theory because it would contend human freedom to be delusional and define human happiness as freedom from anxiety. According to Freud, freedom is seen not in terms of willing or doing but rather as a kind of mental state, unencumbered by incapacitating anxiety. According to Freud, the individual's sense of willing and free participation in one's own choices is really a myth, since everyone is unavoidably shackled to one's personal and cultural past. McAdams describes Freud's deterministic philosophy as follows:

According to Freud and the psychoanalytic tradition all significant behavior and experience is determined by forces over which we have little control. Although those forces
come both from within the person and from the outside world psychoanalysts are typically most interested in the internal impulses that shape a person's life. The most significant internal forces are instincts, (sometimes called "drives" from the German *Trieb*). . . .
Instincts, therefore, function as bridges linking the biology and the psychology of the
person. They are the mechanisms by which the biological energy of the person is translated into psychological form. As such, instincts are the fundamental motivators of human actions.[3]

If human beings can successfully avoid pain and gain pleasure, they are doing OK as far as human nature goes. In 1929, ten years before his death, Freud
wrote the following:

We will. . . turn to the. . . question of what men themselves show by their behavior to be
the purpose and intention of their lives. What do they demand of life and wish to achieve
in it? The answer to this can hardly be in doubt. They strive after happiness; they want
to become happy and to remain so. This endeavor has two sides: a positive and a negative aim. It aims, on the one hand, at the absence of pain and unpleasure, and, on the
other, at the experiencing of strong feelings of pleasure. In its narrower sense the word
'happiness' only relates to the last. In conformity with this dichotomy in his aims, man's
activity develops in two directions, according as it seeks to realize—in the main, or even
exclusively—the one or the other of these aims.[4]

All other seemingly constructive activity such as science, art, and literature
are just products of various mechanisms humans have invented to protect humanity from anxiety. Through defense mechanisms of sublimation, compensation, and reaction formation, it is possible to disguise one's sense of failure,
weakness, or guilt and become, perchance, a competent scientist, writer, or artist—but only by way of defense. As Norman O. Brown writes in his book *Life
Against Death: The Psychoanalytical Meaning of History*, "The link between
psychoanalysis and the science of human culture is the concept of sublimation.
If psychoanalysis is right, virtually the totality of what anthropologists call culture consists of sublimations. Freud not only regards higher mental operations,
such as scientific, artistic and ideological activities as sublimation's of sexual
energy, but also the less high but more fundamental cultural activity of work."[5]

The sociologist Richard LaPiere deplores the consequences of Freud's doctrine by making reference to what he terms the "Freudian ethic."[6]

But how do we account for its success if it is so deterministic in its conception of human nature? Its fatalism is its most seductive feature, since it elimi-
nates personal responsibility and expiates guilt. Indeed, the burdensome guilt of
the Protestant ethic has been swept away by the ruminations of a Viennese physician. Humanity at last no longer had to feel guilt; no longer were we personally
culpable. And so in this century, humanity sought a new beginning and found
determinism. We desired freedom and traded it for fatalism.

Peter Gay, a Freud biographer and scholar, makes the following chilling
comparisons: "Copernicus had shown that the earth, and hence man, is not the

center of the universe; Darwin had linked mankind to the animal kingdom, and now he, Freud, had demonstrated that reason is not master in its own house."[7]

Gay emphatically states in the opening sentence of the preface to *The Freud Reader* that "Sigmund Freud—along with Karl Marx, Charles Darwin, and Albert Einstein—is among the small handful of supreme makers of the twentieth-century mind whose works should be our prized possession."[8] In fairness to the Freudian tradition, it does indeed provide many brilliant insights and if not taken as a total view of human nature, can be instructive and useful. As Gay says Freud is "inescapable." It is, however, devastating as the moral philosophy it has become. In Freud's words; "what decides the purpose of life is simply the programme of the pleasure principle."[9]

Freud's ideas are disturbing but he must be given his due. His book, *Civilization and Its Discontents* inspired this author to make the following comments about Freud the *artist*:

One can observe in this very interesting document Freud's own conscious processes. I see perhaps two levels of consciousness in the author. One would be Freud's conscious efforts to be analytical, to present, as it were, a scientific treatise. And I am sure Freud would contend that this is indeed a scientific treatise. On the other hand, there is something distinctively nonscientific about the book. It shifts abruptly from image to image and from hypothesis to hypothesis. One can sense within it the workings of a great mind that cannot dismiss an idea once it achieves consciousness because these ideas have been so useful and dependable in the past. I sense, if I may use Freud's own term, Freud's preconscious mind moving throughout the pages—that there is a process going on just below the level of our awareness—that this process parallels the conscious analytical process. It is not scientific. It is much more at an intuitive level. Freud the scientist, the originator of psychoanalytical theory, and Freud the therapist are both collaborating in this work. Freud, after all, always identified himself as a scientist. He began his career as a physiologist and neurologist and spent several years doing laboratory research under the famous physiologist Ernst Brücke. In fact, he postponed his M.D. four years so he could continue with his laboratory research. He clearly expressed a nineteenth century materialism and mechanism in his theorizing and was very heavily influenced by Charles Darwin and Hermann von Helmholtz. On the other hand, he was also a professional therapist who by the age of seventy-three had devoted the last forty years of his life in psychoanalytical psychotherapy with scores of patients. At the height of his practice he was devoting ten to twelve hours a day in psychoanalytical sessions.

For Freud, psychoanalysis was a method, a technique, as Bruno Bettelheim would say, a way of reaching into the soul of a person, not just an abstract theory of personality development. Freud was the compassionate and intuitive artist as much as he was the abstract theoretician. For him, as was equally true of Einstein, intuition and imagination were perhaps more important than theory and fact. Science, after all, seeks closure, it seeks to craft useful paradigms that have conceptual elegance. The artist, on the other hand, avoids closure—the artist needs to feel that at any moment another intuitive leap may occur, another rush of truth. Freud was both the scientist and the artist; both are revealed in this document.[10]

Another major position widely held in psychological circles is traditional behaviorism and related systems known as social learning theory. Traditional behaviorism is based on the original work of John Watson at the beginning of the century.[11] Watson, and later Skinner, insist that human behavior must be understood in terms of natural forces, which are observable and measurable.[12] Their attention focused on the environment as the primary determiner of behavior—a position opposite to Freud's. Behavior was learned through its interaction with the environment. For Skinner, the primary forces in the environment were not Freud's "instincts" but those environmental factors that could reinforce or extinguish behavior. The person as an autonomous being counts for little in Watson's and Skinner's version of behaviorism.

Behaviorism holds that the behaving human is a product of nature and governed by the same natural laws as all other parts of nature. The question for behaviorism is not so much understanding or defining human nature as much as explaining human behavior. The behaviorists contend that unless we observe humans as behaving, we don't observe them at all. All that we necessarily know of human nature must be conceived in terms of human behavior—there is no other way. Therefore, the only legitimate statements we can make about humanity are behavioral ones. To the behaviorist, it makes a great deal of difference whether we say that a person is honest or that the person behaves honestly—or we say that a person is loving or that the person behaves lovingly. Skinner has taken methods to set limits on verifiable knowledge. Such phenomena as soul or will are completely out of reach to a Skinnerian. In fact, they are unnecessary, unverifiable, and indefensible postulates that have hindered rather than facilitated human understanding. One does not explain a complex process such as individual choice by postulating free will any more than one explains natural disasters as acts of God. Skinner takes the position that to the extent that all phenomena are natural, they are knowable. To explain the unknown (or as yet unknown) by postulating the unknowable is from a behavioristic view both unscientific and unforgivable.

Social learning theory, which is an offshoot of the more radical forms of behaviorism proposed by Watson and Skinner, has inserted the person back into its psychological scheme but still insists on the behavioral paradigm of observation and measurement. A leading proponent of social-learning theory is Albert Bandura, who has incorporated cognitive elements into his theorizing (now known as social-cognitive theory).[13] He continues in the tradition of Watson and Skinner but has modified their view on environmental determinism to include person variables such as beliefs and expectancies. He terms his version of determinism *reciprocal determinism*, in which the environment, behavior, and the person interact in ways that have reciprocal influence on each other. By so doing, Bandura has introduced cognitive (internal) features into a deterministic model—a softened version of determinism, perhaps, but deterministic nonetheless. By Bandura's model we all live in our own kind of *Truman Show* where the power of self is obscured by the controlling features of the world around us. *Time* magazine states the analogy this way:

But like any supple parable, the film allows for several plausible interpretations. It is also about control—the control we try to exercise over ourselves and others, using stratagems of love, hope and fear. Most people think they have something to do with shaping their existence. But what if that's a fiction? Who's directing our lives? And how do we negotiate with God or fate or the great TV auteur in the sky? Finally, the film speaks to man's isolation from the world around him. The solipsist believes that he is the only reality; everything else is just. . . TV.[14]

Contrasted with deterministic positions in psychology is the humanistic-existential view that the human being is essentially free to choose his or her own way in life. Modern humanistic psychology finds its roots in existential philosophy and its chief proponents, Kierkegaard, Heidegger, Sartre, and others. The existential argument is eloquently expressed by Sartre when he contends that a human's existence precedes essence.[15] According to Sartre, human beings create their own essences. For the existentialist, the human dilemma is the fact of existence and nonexistence. Human beings, aware of the fact that someday they will cease to exist, are faced with the crisis of existence/nonexistence. The question for the existentialist is that all people must define their own essence. We do this out of our own resources as human beings; we do so freely and creatively. To live a meaningful and rewarding life for the existentialist depends upon every person's capacity to shape his or her own essence. It is this process that gives life its vitality and character. Although the specter of death and nothingness lends gloom to the existential position, Sartre argues that it is not a pessimistic philosophy because it centers in human freedom and every person's capacity to decide to be. To this extent he is right, at least to the extent that existentialism is not a deterministic philosophy.

Psychologists have come to similar conclusions as the existentialists, especially as a result of their efforts in counseling and psychotherapy. Notably, Carl Rogers in the United States and Viktor Frankl in Europe, both psychotherapists, have argued the essential freedom in being human. Humanistic psychology sees each person not as a necessary and irrevocable product of upbringing and environment but rather as an individual capable of growth and adjustment. Humanistic psychology places confidence in our capacity for growth and becoming—to achieve new dimensions of living by actualizing our potential as free, competent, and creative human beings.

The humanistic psychotherapist resists the medical model, which looks for causes. Rather, there is acceptance of each person as here and now, alive, in need, capable of becoming anew and achieving a new plateau of existence. This capacity exists in all people by virtue of their humanity, and their humanity is exercised, indeed realized, by each person's free choice to actuate one's potential—potential to love, to create, to find meaning in work and in sharing.

Leaders such as Allport, Maslow, Rogers, and Frankl have moved psychological thought out of the laboratory and into the arena of life. For them, psychology is less an examination of behavior and more a study of life itself. As Allport has stated, "Not every brand—indeed no single brand—of modern psychology is wholly adequate to the problem of man's individuality and growth."[16]

To the behaviorist, life is operationally defined as a range of behavior. To the psychoanalyst, life is the channeling of biologic and psychic energy. To the existential humanist, life is power to grow, to be, and to love. Life is constantly achieving new levels and forms of becoming. Life is never static, never determined, never stable enough for precise observation and controlled study. Life is worth living. Human life is to live completely, not in morbid preoccupation with the past, not in resigned acceptance of causal forces, but rather, futuristically and courageously. Moreover, each person's life is totally one's own to do with what one wishes. Such ownership is beyond inquiry and definition. Such is the ownership Sartre implies in his notion that all humans decide their own essence. It is the ownership Rollo May describes when referring to the testimony of a San Quentin prisoner as interviewed by the psychologist Philip Zimbardo.

Out of unspeakably degrading and cruel conditions in solitary confinement, in what with strange irony is called a "Maximum Adjustment Center," this prisoner, who seems to be a Chicano and something of a poet, spoke as follows:

They have separated me from my family; deprived me of touching my young boy; taken away every material possession; hidden the sun, moon and stars from my view; exchanged their concrete and steel for earth and flowers and everything warm and soft. . . . They have left me with nothing, nothing except an inner core, a secret, private place they have not yet found how to get to.

It is where I think of who I am, try to understand the what and why of my enemies, and where I keep alive my will to live in a hell where I am made to feel like a nothing, at best an animal, a wild animal in captivity.

Although I sometimes get depressed and feel like giving up, the discovery of my self and my thoughts gives me joy, for until they find a way to take my thoughts away, I am free. A man can live without liberty but not without freedom. Knowledge is freedom and becomes the source of hope in this most hopeless of all places.[17]

WILLING

The existentialist view that each person is a responsible, cogent being says a great deal about the nature of humanity. Our humanity is our freedom and we become complete to the extent that we function freely—that we move heart and mind in directions compatible with our human nature.

The danger in the Freudian ethic is that it undermines individual freedom and human responsibility. In fact, a great deal of harm has already been wrought by Freud and the psychoanalytical school of thought. Thomas S. Szasz writes: "The concept of personal responsibility is central to the concept of man as moral agent. Without it, individual freedom, Western man's most cherished value becomes a 'denial of reality,' a veritable 'psychotic delusion' to endow man with a grandeur he does not in fact possess."[18] The twentieth century may go down in history as the age of skepticism in humanity's essential value. In the words of

Richard LaPiere, "Freudianism is a doctrine of social irresponsibility and personal despair."[19]   This philosophy has slowly (but surely) permeated the culture of Western civilization. With behaviorism as cohort, Freudian psychology has set the stage for a postmodern view of the self as indeterminant, as constantly being redefined by those myriad social forces in which it is embedded. In this sense the postmodern self lacks unity as a self-directed personal agency.

To offset the dilution of self as a viable concept, any theory of human motivation must necessarily confront human freedom. It must either deny or affirm the possibility that we can decide the path of our own existence. We have seen that psychoanalysis and behaviorism deny this capacity. To the Freudian or to the behaviorist, free will is both a myth and an unnecessary postulate for life. Their view is that we can have an adequate psychology built on scientific principles without the need for free will. Allport feels otherwise: "How wrong we have been in viewing the process of growth as a reaction to past and present stimuli, neglecting the dynamics of futurity; of orientation, intention and valuation."[20]

Willing is more distinctive of humanity than thinking. It is by virtue of our will that we are distinctly human. Therefore, we experience our unique selfhood and our humanity when exercising free choice, when goals are set and decisions are made, when we act upon reality freely and willingly. The postmodern person feels depleted because there are forces at work resulting in a loss in the ability to choose and to decide. Unless humanity decides to be, humanity will cease to be. If life is worth living, we must decide that it is so, postmodernism notwithstanding. If the human race is worth preserving, we must decide to do so. Our future rests in our decision to continue to exist.

To will is to be, and to be is to will. And it is in exercising the will that each human becomes empowered as a person. In willing, the person experiences potency in a way not otherwise possible. The human being senses reality and nature when making a true decision. Decision making is a most important feature of living a full life. Unfortunately, however, the modern person is being divested of decision making ability by both technology and by an exaggerated emphasis on group process. Technology, like one huge cookbook, provides recipes at all levels of life so that probabilities are so well established that the individual no longer decides but simply assesses and reacts.   Probability statements in the media become a substitute for critical judgment, and one is divested of the power of choice. Increasingly, decisions are being made for us by technology. The impact of the Internet is not yet fully realized, but the mass marketing of ideas that come from many unchallenged sources can confuse the acts of critical judgment and decision making. More and more, human individuality is being digitalized by that giant computer in the sky. A sense of uniqueness as a person is certainly being diminished in our postmodern times. Also, to gain reassurance regarding the reliability of our feelings and perceptions, we turn to our fellow humans and willingly reveal our most intimate feelings in a process group of some sort.[21] Human beings need to know that other human beings have experiences and emotions like their own—that other people experience pain, fear, guilt, and uncertainty. There is no question that group activity facilitates our sense of personal assurance and enhances perceptivity of others. What is at risk, however, is the individual deciding for and of oneself to be one's own person and to choose one's own way in life. There is great value in a sense of "we," and frequently, problems are more readily solved by group involvement, but there is also great value in "I" and each person's ability to decide and to experience one's power as a person.

We should not underestimate the importance of human decision making. The individual's sense of worth and value are a direct result of acts of willing and deciding—yes, as a free, self-determining human being. The theory of human motivation proposed in this book rests in the conviction not only that the person is free but that human freedom defines human nature.[22]

THE FUNCTIONAL AUTONOMY OF MOTIVES

We know from our earlier discussion that motivational theory and psychology in general owe a great deal to the pioneering thought of Gordon Allport at Harvard. Allport's ideas were remarkable for their time because they ran counter to Freud's great "discoveries." Allport said that human motives were not necessarily determined by earlier events but could become functionally free from their originating conditions. Allport called his theory *the functional autonomy of motives*.[23] Allport also insisted that each person had to be understood in terms of one's uniqueness as an individual. He has stated it this way: "I venture the opinion that all of the animals in the world are psychologically less distinct from one another than one man is from other men."[24] To attempt to understand individual motivation in terms of common human experiences, therefore, would inevitably miss the mark. He felt that each person had to be understood as an individual, and that each person's motivations were one's own as a unique person. Allport said that if you want to know something about a person, "why not first ask." This view was quite remarkable in an age in which the Freudian doctrine of unconscious motivation was so widely accepted. Allport was a great believer in human consciousness. It was his view that the human being consciously participates in personal acts—that motives could be conscious, present in time, and centered in human awareness and responsibility. Functional autonomy of motives, therefore, refers to the fact that motives occur independently from earlier causes—that at any point in time, human motives can be autonomous and not a function of the past. An example would be athletes who excel in sports because they enjoy sports and not because they are compensating for personal inadequacies in other areas of life.

Theories of unconscious motivation would argue that a person excels in sports as a compensation for a personal sense of deficiency in another important life area; athletic prowess, therefore, is determined by earlier unconscious motives. In this case, the defense mechanism is compensation—the ego protects itself from painful anxiety by compensating for inadequacy in one life area by excelling in another. However, Allport said that the individual's interest in sports can become *functionally autonomous* from earlier conditions so that the person excels in golf not because of compensation, but because of an active and present interest in golf, or fishing, or whatever the sport may be. The decision, therefore, to improve one's golf game is a free, conscious decision. Likewise, the research chemist is motivated by a conscious interest in the subject and not because he or she is unconsciously trying to please mother by intellectual achievements his or her father was incapable of.

Allport did not categorically reject Freudian thinking, but he felt that it falls far short of the complete story. Allport's emphasis on the individual and consciousness was an extremely important position against the psychoanalytical tide of thought and a key factor in preserving humanity's sense of freedom and dignity among personality theorists.

Personality, therefore, can be regarded as an internal patterning of individual motives. Motives do not stem from personality. It is quite the opposite. It is the cumulation and patterning of motives over time that make up the phenomenon we call personality.

A LARGER PERSPECTIVE

From a psychological standpoint, not all causation is fixed in past events. If one establishes a purpose in life, that purpose will influence the present and will place limits on the effects of the past. For example, if Angela decides that she wants to use her talents to become an accomplished violinist, this will change the way she structures her current activities. Her operational motivations (those that occur in the present) will change to complement her new life purpose. She will likely decide to devote more time to practicing. She may want to attend more musical events and earn extra money to do so. She may add more literature on music to her readings. She may want to invest some of her savings toward the purchase of a new violin, make new friends, and so on. Also, her new sense of commitment to her music and optimistic plans for the future will limit the effects of past life experiences, which may have had a negative influence on her (formative motivation). If, for example, she tended to get depressed from time to time, her newfound optimism may inhibit her depression.

Daniel Goleman in his book *Emotional Intelligence* frequently refers to the work of psychologist Martin Seligman and his research on optimism at the University of Pennsylvania. Goleman has this to say about optimism: "Optimism, like hope, means having a strong expectation that, in general, things will turn out all right in life, despite setbacks and frustrations. From the standpoint of emotional intelligence, optimism is an attitude that buffers people against falling into apathy, helplessness or depression in the face of tough going."[25]

His quote from Seligman gets to the importance of thematic motivation.

For the last thirty or forty years we've seen the ascendance of individualism and a waning of larger beliefs in religion, and in supports from the community and extended family.

That means a loss of resources that can buffer you against setbacks and failures. To the extent you see a failure as something that is lasting and which you magnify to taint everything in your life, you are prone to let a momentary defeat become a lasting source of hopelessness. But if you have a larger perspective, like a belief in God and an after-life, and you lose your job, it's just a temporary defeat.[26]

The "larger perspective" Seligman speaks about could be called conviction, an important psychological process tied to thematic motivation.

The word *conviction* carries two components—one cognitive, the other emotional. When conviction exists, both components are equally present—one is mind and the other is heart. To form a conviction in life is to build an important new set of assumptions and beliefs about ourselves and our futures. Optimism about the future also carries with it a strong emotional component that provides us with the drive and perseverance to make our convictions work.

Conviction is a powerful word. It involves mind and heart working together to make something important happen in our lives. A life without convictions may be less resistant to negative feelings of emptiness and hopelessness. Our convictions put us in charge of our futures. They energize us and give us direction. They contribute to a sense of optimism in the future.

Optimism is what Goleman calls "The Great Motivator."[27]

NOTES

1. Richard Corliss, "Smile! Your Life's on TV," *Time*, 1 June 1998, 78.
2. Sigmund Freud, *Basic Writings of Sigmund Freud* (New York: Modern Library, 1938).
3. Dan P. McAdams, 66 (see chap. 1, n. 1).
4. Sigmund Freud, *Civilization and Its Discontents*, trans. and ed. James Strachey (New York: W. W. Norton & Co., 1961), 24.
5. Norman J. O. Brown, *Life Against Death, The Psychoanalytical Meaning of History* (New York: Random House, 1959), 135.
6. Richard LaPiere, *The Freudian Ethic* (New York: Duell, Sloan and Pearch, 1959).
7. Peter Gay, *The Freud Reader* (New York: W. W. Norton & Co., 1989), xvii.
8. Ibid., x.
9. Freud, *Civilization and Its Discontents*, 24.
10. Robert Cavalier, "Freud's Civilization and Its Discontents," Dana Lecture Series, Elmira College, March 1989.
11. John B. Watson, *Behaviorism* (New York: W. W. Norton & Co., 1925).
12. B. F. Skinner, *About Behaviorism* (New York: Alfred A. Knopf, 1974).
13. Albert Bandura, "The Self System in Reciprocal Determinism," *American Psychologist* 33 (1978), 344–358.
14. Corliss, "Smile! Your Life's on TV," 79.

15. Jean Paul Sartre, *Existentialism and Human Emotions* (New York: Philosophical Library, 1957).

16. Gordon W. Allport, *Becoming: Basic Considerations for a Psychology of Personality* (New Haven: Yale University Press, 1955), 5.

17. Rollo May, "Freedom, Determinism and the Future," *Psychology*, trial issue (April 1977), 8.

18. Thomas S. Szasz, *Ideology and Insanity: Essays on the Psychiatric Dehumanization of Man.* (Garden City, NY: Doubleday, 1970), 11. Thomas Szasz, perhaps more than any other writer, has attacked the psychoanalytical school of thought as it has been nourished and advanced over the years, especially by the psychiatric profession. Szasz, who is himself a psychiatrist, has accused psychiatry of depreciating human values by placing the whole person within the artificial and inherently damaging constraints of diagnostic categories and labels. According to Szasz, psychiatry, in following the master, Sigmund Freud, has perpetrated a great injustice on patients seeking help and understanding. Instead of dealing with individuals in terms of their uniqueness and individuality, instead of relating on a subjective and personal basis, psychiatry has remained objective and diagnostic, applying a medical approach whereby those seeking help are classified as mentally sick, then given a diagnosis according to symptoms and assigned a psychiatric label. They are then treated as one would treat a patient with a broken arm. The treatment, of course, should ultimately result in a cure. Szasz has said that this lack of compassion and concern for the humanity of the person has left the person alone, isolated, fearful, and misunderstood, and has, in fact, produced more harm than good.

19. LaPiere, *The Freudian Ethic*, 53.

20. Allport, *Becoming*, 76.

21. A "process group" is one that is brought together to facilitate the personal development of its members. Through group interaction, members become more aware of their own feelings and how their behavior impacts others. Sensitivity groups, encounter groups, and counseling groups are examples of "process" groups.

22. Many writers no longer see human nature in terms of personal freedom, and the concept of will has been overshadowed by our preoccupation with human cognition and intelligence. Although experiments with animals have encroached upon our special ability to think abstractly, we nonetheless continue to exalt human nature for its ability to reason and to think. We have, in fact, defined the human as homo sapiens—*sapiens* meaning *knowing* or *wise*.

23. Gordon W. Allport, *Personality: A Psychological Interpretation* (New York: Henry Holt and Co., 1937).

24. Allport, *Becoming*, 23.

25. Goleman, 88 (see chap. 1, n. 13).

26. Ibid., 241.

27. Ibid., 87.

CHAPTER 3

Nature and Freedom

The thoughts themselves are the thinkers.

—William James, *Psychology: The Briefer Course* (p. 83)

Immanuel Kant, one of the world's great philosophers, never traveled beyond forty miles of his birthplace in the eighty years of his life, yet his thoughts have influenced generations of scholars and continue to do so two hundred years after his death. As a professor of philosophy at the University of Köningsberg in Germany, he lived quietly and peacefully in his own thoughts and never deviated from his daily routine. "Kant was more punctual and more precise than the town clocks of Köningsberg. His habits were steadfast and unchangeable. Passersby in Köningsberg regulated their watches whenever they saw Herr Professor Doktor Immanuel Kant on his daily stroll."[1] Kant was fascinated with human rationality, and in his book *Critique of Pure Reason,* he argues that certain "categories" of thought exist *a priori*, that is, that the human mind by its very nature possesses certain essential first principles of thought. *Causation,* he argued was one of these first principles.[2]

Causation is perhaps the first feature of human thought, through which all knowledge depends. Without causation, it would be impossible to engage in human reasoning or acquire any kind of knowledge. Human reason is inextricably connected to the idea of causation, which for most is a self-evident principle whereby we observe and reason about the world and conduct our life's business.

But once you get past the obvious into the realms of philosophy and psychology, causation gets to be a tricky idea. All science depends upon the principle of causation, which it calls determinism. From the point of view of science, the understanding, control, and prediction of natural phenomena depend upon causation. (John Watson once asserted that the objective of psychology was to predict and control behavior.) But Aristotle did not view causation as a simple linear process and proposed four different causes, for everything that exists: the material cause, the formal cause, the efficient cause and the final cause. The material cause is the actual matter that makes up an object. For example, a bridge is constructed from concrete and steel. The formal cause is the shape or form of the bridge as the engineers have designed it; the bridge was constructed according to a design, which is its formal cause. The efficient cause is the work in building the bridge as supplied by the construction team. And the final cause is the purpose for which the bridge is built. Every bridge ever built was constructed with a purpose in mind.

We think of Aristotle's final cause as the purpose for which an object exists, and it is this cause that has created the greatest problem for science, because modern science would reject the idea that there is any design or plan in the universe. Psychology, under the influence of Darwinian natural selection and Watsonian behaviorism, would concur. According to enlightened science, especially since Darwin, all events are moved along by previous events without rhyme or reason but simply as these events become selected by nature. All organisms, humans included, are the result of this natural selection process. Organisms survive only because they have the ability to survive in a particular environment ("survival of the fittest") and hence are adaptable. That is, they are able to pass their genes to future members of the species. Those members of the species who are unable to cope with the environment (which may include humans as predators) eventually become extinct. Many species large and small are earmarked for extinction unless a significant change in the environment allows them to survive, including the human predator and the pollution humans produce.

For example, during the Industrial Revolution in late nineteenth-century England, a particular light colored moth was replaced by a dark colored related moth as the prevalent variety. Why? Industrial pollution had blackened the forests, improving the darker moth's camouflage against predators such as birds. The light colored moth became too visible to predators to survive. Recently, however, with restrictions on air pollution, the light moth is making a comeback. Thus, natural selection is a constantly shifting process, influenced by an organism's demands of the environment.[3]

According to the logic of natural selection and hence modern science, humans occupy the world as a result of pure chance without design or destiny, and human behavior is best understood as taking its particular shape (shaping is a behaviorist term consistent with Aristotle's formal cause) as a result of natural selective processes.[4] Human intelligence and reason must be the result of these natural selection forces (Aristotle's efficient cause). Human freedom and human will are not part of this deterministic model. Willing and human intentions that result in purposeful behavior are somehow not accounted for in the Darwinian plan of things. To decide, to intend, and to will imply some kind of purpose or plan and is consistent with Aristotle's final cause, which science rejects. How planful and deciding humans fit into a non-planful world has challenged deterministic logic. How a product of nature seems to do that which nature cannot do is a remarkable paradox, after all, the behaviorist B. F. Skinner produces the behavior he intends his pigeons to demonstrate. In so doing, he uses a reinforcement model, and he is content to explain human intentions within the same model.[5]

I KNOW THAT I KNOW THAT I KNOW

Joseph Rychlak in his book *Artificial Intelligence and Human Reason* argues for a psychology of free will and opposes those theoretical psychologists who see all human faculties as machine-like systems. For these psychologists, all psychological processes can be explained in terms of Aristotle's material and efficient causes. Aristotle's formal and final causes are not only not applicable to mechanistic logic, but they are seen as depreciating what can be known by strictly objective and external observation. The mechanists refuse to accept an internal self as an independent knowing agency. These theoreticians see the self as some sort of subsystem within an artificial intelligence model that can be understood on the basis of neurological networks and feedback loops of one form or another. "Indeed 'the self' as a concept is viewed as nothing but a linguistic convention, a learned symbol. . . . "[6] D. R. Hofstadter states his position as follows:

My belief is that the explanations of "emergent" phenomena in our brains—for instance, ideas, hopes, images, and finally consciousness and free will—are based on a kind of Strange Loop, an interaction between levels in which the top level reaches back down toward the bottom level and influences it, while at the same time being itself determined by the bottom level. The self comes into being at the moment it has the power to reflect itself.[7]

All of our higher human faculties are accounted for in this way—a way that is inherently mechanistic and devoid of any planful or purposeful content as would be seen from the inside out. Hofstadter's view of the self is looking at it from the outside in and the "power to reflect itself" is a mechanical, indeed a determining kind of efficient power. The internal content of self, what we all experience as thinkers, dreamers, and planners, is somehow explained as reflection upon oneself. How this explains mental content in its myriad forms remains mysterious. More mysterious is how reflection explains intentional behavior, the ability to shift goals, or stop an action once started. For Hofstadter, free will is a feeling as much as anything else. "From this balance between self-knowledge and self-ignorance comes the feeling of free will."[8]

Rychlak states the following: "Suffice it to say that in this [Hofstadter's] entire theoretical development there is no introspective formulation, and hence, no real way in which to describe the self of being reflexively cognizant of the fact that 'it' is the predicator of what will be known, of what knowledge means or what will count as knowledge to enlighten the unknown."[9]

Rychlak agrees with William James that there is a self as knower.

The I, or 'pure ego' is . . . the *Thinker*; and the question immediately comes up *what* is the thinker? Is it the passing state of consciousness itself, or is it something deeper and less mutable? The passing state we have seen to be the very embodiment of change. . . . Yet each of us spontaneously considers that by 'I' he means something always the same. This has led most philosophers to postulate behind the passing state of consciousness a permanent Substance or Agent whose modification or act it is. This Agent is the thinker; the 'state' is only its instrument or means. 'Soul' 'transcental Ego', 'Spirit,' are so many names for this more permanent sort of Thinker.[10]

Philosophers have greater latitude in dealing with this problem than psychologists, (especially behavioral and cognitive psychologists who are bound by determinism.) "To know that I know" and "to know that I know that I know" is found in the same self that "wills that it wills" and "wills that it wills that it wills." Such a self is a real entity that really knows and really wills.

MEASURING THINGS

That we, as humans, possess free will is scientific psychology's biggest bugaboo. Science necessarily espouses determinism, and therefore, psychology, which claims to be a science, must also insist on determinism. Determinism contends that any knowable natural occurrence can be understood as caused by other knowable natural occurrences. (This is also referred to as positivism.) Nothing exists without some cause, which becomes the business of science to make knowable. Why heat transfers from a hot grill to become hot water can be understood by science. Why water converts to steam at a given temperature under given atmospheric pressure is also known by science. Temperature and atmospheric pressure can both be measured precisely. Science therefore is intimately connected to measurement, which really makes science possible. Measurements that are objective and precise give science its validity and its reliability from place to place and from scientist to scientist. Thus twentieth-century psychology has become preoccupied with the development of objective measures of psychological processes, whatever they may be. Intelligence testing is an example, as is the electroencephalogram (EEG) as a measure of brain wave patterns. Psychology uses many other examples, and all psychologists are trained in psychological statistics and research design and methods. Even humanistic and philosophically minded psychologists must sweat out courses in statistics and perform research investigations to earn their advanced degrees. Because psychology is a science, there are no exceptions to this, at least not in psychology programs accredited by the American Psychological Association. American psychology, in fact, has its origins in scientific research and the development of quantifiable data. This is what made psychology separate from philosophy and resulted in the establishment of psychology departments in a few American universities before the turn of the century. One of the best examples is the psychology laboratory begun at Cornell University in 1892 by the Englishman, Edward Bradford Titchener. "Titchener ruled his domain with an iron fist. He determined what the research projects would be and which students would work on them. For him psychology was experimental psychology (as he defined it); and everything that preceded his version of psychology was not psychology at all."[11] It is interesting to note that although Titchener excluded women from a scientific society he founded because he felt they "might be offended by the excessive cigar smoke at the meetings,"[12] his first doctoral candidate was Margaret Floy Washburn, who, in June 1894, became the first woman ever to receive a doctorate in psychology. (Harvard, on the other hand, refused a doctorate to Mary Whiton Calkins in 1895, although William James described her performance on her unofficial doctoral examination as the "best he had ever seen at Harvard.")[13]

The first Ph.D. in psychology was awarded to G. Stanley Hall by Harvard University in 1878. His doctoral thesis was "The Muscular Perception of Space." Hall became the "great graduate teacher of American Psychology. By 1893 eleven of the fourteen Ph.D. degrees from American universities had been given by him; by 1898 this had increased to thirty awarded out of fifty-four."[14] And although psychology successfully shed philosophy and progressed as a science during this century, determinism and free will are still debatable ideas. If, as many believe, humans possess free will, and if free will defines human nature, then what is essentially most true of humans is out of the reach of empirical science. For centuries, thinkers have struggled with this paradox and have tried to resolve it in different ways. B. F. Skinner, regarded by many as this century's greatest psychologist, simply set the paradox aside and started his case for a science of psychology built on demonstrable data. In fact, Skinner went so far as to reject psychological theory entirely since theory can reflect subjective biases. Skinner shared with Titchener the positivist view that psychological knowledge should be based only on demonstrable data, preferably generated in a psychological laboratory. (Titchener used human participants, whereas Skinner is famous for his work with pigeons.)

IS LIFE LEARNED BEHAVIOR?

The ability to learn is but one of several attributes of the living person. A psychology, therefore, that focuses on learned behavior offers only a partial understanding of the problem of living and can offer only partial solutions. Some attributes of biopsychological life are:

1.   consciousness
2.   evolution

3. growth and maturation
4. generativity
5. regenerativity (healing)
6. homeostasis
7. adaptation
8. learning and knowing
9. thinking and reasoning
10. curiosity and creativity
11. intending and deciding
12. motivation
13. volition
14. ownership and selfhood
15. identity and differentiation
16. loving and nurturing
17. decline and death

Learning bears upon many of these attributes to some degree, but clearly, living is more than simply "learned behavior." Behavior may be an attribute of life, but behavior does not define life any more than color defines a Van Gogh painting. To say that a Van Gogh is colorful does not define a Van Gogh. There is harmony, inner relationship, strength, character and many other attributes of a Van Gogh that taken together fail to define a Van Gogh. In fact, all the attributes of a great painting taken together do not define a painting. The painting must be seen. Art must be understood in holistic terms. The same is true of life. Life is inner relationship, life is harmony, life is capacity to reproduce one's own kind. Life is growth. Living beings grow, age, heal themselves, and reproduce themselves. They evolve, constantly adapt, and change.

All humans participate in life. They are conceived; they develop; they grow, mature, age, decline, and ultimately die. None of these phenomenon is learned behavior. Growth is not behavior. Healing is not behavior. Aging is not behavior, although there are behaviors that can hasten or delay death.. Also, life reproduces itself. This capacity to reproduce one's own kind is not defined by sexual activity. Procreative power is not behavior. Human potential is not behavior.

Living beings evolve into new forms. Human nature consists of all the above, yet none of the above can be defined as behavior per se. To be sure, growth and aging are manifested in myriad behaviors, but the processes of evolving, growing, and aging are not behavior. Certainly, empirical psychology falls far short of defining human nature.

A MANIFESTATION OF NATURE

The presence of a microbe in a piece of planetary debris discovered in Canada in August 1996 shook the world as evidence that extraterrestrial life may indeed exist. If true, this is a fascinating discovery that suggests many possibilities, including the fact that our own life may have been transported to earth from another planet many millions of years ago. But such a discovery in a piece of planetary rock is hardly life as studied by social science, much less the life reported by *Time* magazine as the "Miracle of Iowa" in its account of the birth of seven children to Bobbie McCaughey on November 19, 1997."[15] The birth of seventy fingers and seventy toes is a miracle far more meaningful than the discovery of "possible life" in a piece of planetary rock. The courage of the babies' mother says a great deal about human nature, and how we can fulfill our destiny as a people on this planet regardless of our primordial origins—even if on another planet.

To say that humanity is a part of nature doesn't really say very much about being human. A ball point pen is a part of nature, too. Skinner says that "man is much more than a dog, but like a dog he is within the range of a scientific analysis."[16] In this sense a dog and a man (or an elephant or a pigeon for that matter) although different, are both parts of nature and subject to the laws of nature—hence within the range of scientific analysis. Although it is impossible to refute Skinner on this point, his statement about a dog and a man clearly indicate the dangerous reductionism of the behavioral approach to understanding human nature. We certainly do not need scientific analysis to observe that humanity has produced literature, art, music, buildings, cities, and rocket ships as well as wars, pollution, prisons, and electric chairs and that dogs have done none of these things.   Is not this difference in itself important, scientific analysis notwithstanding? Is not humanity's uniqueness really more important than the similarity humans bear with the rest of nature. Mozart's greatness is not a function of comparable natural parts he shares with a dog, but can be understood and appreciated only within the uniqueness of the person himself. We understand Mozart best not by subjecting him to scientific analysis, but by listening to his music.

In this sense, then, a human being, a dog, or a pigeon are best understood not as parts but rather as *manifestations of nature*, and there is a considerable and significant difference in this distinction.

Nature necessarily manifests itself in various forms, all of which are "natural" and all of which taken together make up nature. In fact, one cannot think of nature except as manifested in its various forms. An analogy would be a poem or a painting as manifestations of art. Although you may refer to a poem or a painting as a "work of art," one does not understand the poem, the painting, or art, for that matter, by referring to them this way. When, however, we read a poem or view a painting, we can begin to understand how that which is art is manifested through them, although the poem or the painting share very little in common. And so it is with nature. Nature is manifest through humanity, forests, lakes, planets, dogs, and pigeons. Human beings, planets and pigeons are vastly different manifestations of nature, and to know a lot about one helps only a little in knowing anything about the other. By the same token, knowing a great deal about Shakespeare's work is of little help in knowing anything about Beethoven's music or Michelangelo's paintings. Poetry, music, and painting are different. Different principles apply to each and no amount of scientific analysis can ever eradicate the differences that exist. So, too, human beings, planets, and pigeons are different, and various natural principles account for each.

It is, therefore, better (much better and much more useful) to think of humanity not merely as a product of nature but as a manifestation of nature—perhaps nature's most fascinating manifestation since humanity is possessed with the highest attributes of nature—creativity and freedom. To view humanity as a "product" of nature means that we can understand humanity better by understanding nature better. But it could be vice versa. Perhaps natural science can learn more about nature by having social science provide information about our humanness. After all, what's true of humans must also be true of nature itself. A careful study of humanity should by this logic provide interesting leads into nature. We tend not to think of consciousness, freedom, and intelligence as attributes of nature, but perhaps we should begin to do so.[17] Philosophers have been intrigued by the idea that what is true of humanity must be true of nature itself and that the best way to understand nature is to understand what makes us human. Human reasoning, for example, has produced mathematics and mathematical proofs. However, the Pythagoreans believed that mathematics had an independent existence intrinsic to all of nature.[18] Morton Wagman has informed us that "Heinrick Hertz, who developed the theory and technology of radio waves, asserted that electromagnetic wave phenomena were best understood as mathematical equations and like Pythagoras, believed that mathematics had an intrinsic intelligence of its own that sometimes surpasses its creators."[19]

In his discussion of intelligence and nature, Wagman provides some other interesting ideas:

It is of interest that Sir Arthur Stanley Eddington (1882–1944). . . . hypothesized that because knowledge of the universe is the product of the human mind discovery of the nature of the mechanics of the human mind would enable purely conceptual procedures to formulate the entire science of physics. Eddington constructed his hypothesis long before developments in cognitive psychology and artificial intelligence resulted in specific knowledge of the operations of the human mind. These advances in cognitive science have impressed the eminent theoretical physicist Stephen Hawking to further Eddington's hypothesis and turn it in the unexpected direction wherein computer programs rather than human minds create theoretical physics.[20]

If Eddington's or Hawking's position is valid, then truth would work its way backward from human intelligence to nature itself. Cognitive science is, after all, more a part of social science than natural science and Wagman, who wrote the book quoted here, is a psychologist. This is compatible with the ideas of the philosophy of Immanuel Kant mentioned at the beginning of this chapter. Kant states: "Our intellect does not draw its laws from nature but imposes its laws on nature."[21]

FREEDOM, ART AND SPIRIT

What of human freedom? If human freedom is an essential quality of human life, indeed of human nature, how can any behaviorist argument refute it? The question is whether human freedom is beyond the natural limits of scientific investigation. William James offered his caveat one hundred years ago when he wrote in his classic text *Psychology* that speculation about human freedom is really more a matter of philosophy than it is psychology.

For ourselves we can hand the free-will controversy over to metaphysics. Psychology will surely never grow refined enough to discover, in the case of any individual's decision, a descrepancy between his scientific calculations and the fact. His prevision will never foretell, whether the effort be completely predestinate or not, the way in which each individual emergency is resolved. Psychology will be psychology, and Science, science, as much as ever (as much and no more) in this world, whether free-will be true in it or not.[22]

Skinner, Freud, and others who, as psychologists, reject the idea of human freedom have ignored James's admonition. Moreover, it would seem that the burden of proof is not on those who accept human freedom but on those who reject it, since our traditions, our mores, and our laws are predicated on the notion of human freedom. The very fact that the word "freedom" exists and has meaning to those who use the word supports the argument that there is such a thing as human freedom. As you cannot use the word "yellow" for a blind person, you cannot use the word "freedom" for a person who has not experienced freedom. Like Thomas Nagel's "Bat," there is something it is like to be a free willing person and we in our subjective experience know how that feels.

For the behaviorist, the lessons of art tells us nothing about human values, since there are no such things. Art cannot tell us anything about human longing since longing is one of those mythical feelings like willing. Indeed, art is useless as a medium of expression because such expression suggests an "autonomous man" within who is doing the expressing. For the behaviorist, a painting is the product of painting behavior—perceptibility, sharpening, learned techniques of medium and color, shading and dimensionality, perspective, and so on, but a painting is no more. It is not a statement of the inner self, since there is no inner self for the behaviorist. Mozart and Beethoven reveal none of their inner selves by their music since they have no inner selves. Remember that for Skinner, "a self is a repertoire of behavior appropriate to a given set of contingencies."[23] The only differences between Mark Twain and William Shakespeare, apart from differences in inherited abilities, are the environmental contingencies that produced two different forms of writing behavior.

And how about the reader, the listener, the viewer of a work of art? Is there anything about their qualities of perception and understanding that reveals their values, their goals, their preferences in living? For the behaviorist, art appreciation is simply another form of behavior that has been learned. The fact that one individual gains more from Picasso than from Renoir says nothing about that person's inner spirit, since there is no inner spirit.

SUBJECTIVITY

One can certainly accept the truths of science but also understand the relativistic and transient aspects of so called "truths." In psychology, there are a few laws as such, although some have been proposed from time to time. Edward Thorndike's Law of Effect (1911) was an important early law for the behaviorists, but no behaviorist would accept Thorndike's law today as he worded it eighty-nine years ago: "Of several responses made to the same situation, those which are accompanied or closely followed by satisfaction to the animal will, other things being equal, be more firmly connected with the situation, so that, when it recurs, they will be more likely to recur."[24] Variable rate reinforcement is generally found to be more effective than continuous reinforcement, and there are individual differences as well. So Thorndike, if not entirely wrong, was not entirely right.

In many psychological studies, method itself can be a problem. The Hawthorne Effect and the Pygmalion Effect both demonstrate how method gets "in the way" of many experiments.[25] On this count, therefore, the scientific-ness of the science of human behavior is questioned, especially when studies involve human participants. Behaviorism, and all of psychology, for that matter, is complicated by the fact that both the subject and object of psychological investigation are the same—the human person, person as investigator, and person as participant. In his book *The Measure of Man*, Joseph Wood Krutch has this to say: "We have been deluded by the fact that methods employed for the study of man have been for the most part those originally devised for the study of machines or the study of rats, and are capable, therefore, of detecting and measuring only those characteristics which the three do have in common."[26]

In this regard B.R. Hergenhahn provides an interesting assessment of the science of psychology. Galileo distinguished between the physical world, later called primary qualities, and the perceived world later called secondary qualities: According to Galileo, science could investigate only the physical world and not the world of perception. "Thus, Galileo excluded from science much of what is now included in psychology, and many modern natural scientists refuse to accept psychology as a science for the same reason that Galileo did not accept it."[27] And although some may argue the cause of freedom and spirit in psychology, these ideas have never left the Galilean psychological arena, all attempts at objectivity notwithstanding. In the March 1998, issue of the American Psychologist, Kirk Schneider in arguing a "science of the heart" makes an important point: "It appears that times have changed in our discipline despite those who still cling to the identification of psychology with hypothetical—deductive—inductive methods. Perhaps the postmodern zeitgeist has brought about an awareness of the limits of an exclusively positivist discipline. . . . Works with philosophical sophistication that address methodological issues and metascientific issues. . . make it more and more difficult to deny the existence of a move toward alternative methods and of numerous legitimate ways to achieve psychological knowledge."[28]

And humanity continues to push forward into vistas unimagined just a few years ago. Space exploration and genetic engineering are two modern examples. Humanity is beginning to approach an infinity identified by Pascal 300 years ago, that infinite distance above and that infinite distance below. Humanity now stands at the threshold to these two infinites.[29]

Ideas cannot be restrained or contained by space or time. The timelessness and transcendence of ideas are beyond any physical person's ability to control or hold. It was Frederick Herbart, perhaps the first educational psychologist, who, in his notion of "apperceptive mass," once proposed that ideas have their own energy.[30] From the point of view of science, there are good ideas and bad ideas. Good ideas are efficient and productive, whereas bad ideas are inefficient and unproductive. But from the point of view of humanity, the value of an idea rests in its force for good, not simply its validity. And so once again we are faced with the issue of human will. To think of a human being as an intelligent animal misses the point completely. And to distinguish humankind from other animals on the basis of intelligence misses the point again.

Humanity already has the brains to survive; the question is, do we have the will to survive? Humanity cannot reason to the preservation of human life, we can only will it. Our reason already has provided us with the capacity to destroy ourselves and it is our will, therefore, that must save us. Decisions are acts of will, not intelligence. This being the case, the fact that humanity has the capacity to decide is an awesome truth indeed. Certainly the differences among Al Capone, Enrico Fermi, and Angelo Roncalli were more matters of will than of intelligence—or would the behaviorists insist as usual that it is a question of environmental contingencies for the three famous Italians? Just think how their personal motives influenced the world.

NOTES

1. Benjamin B. Wolman, ed. "The Historical Roots of Contemporary Psychology," (1968): 229, quoted in B. R. Hergenhahn, *An Introduction to the History of Psychology* (Pacific Grove, Calif: Brooks/Cole, 1997), 168.

2. Immanuel Kant, *Critique of Pure Reason*, trans. N. K. Smith (New York: St. Martin's Press, 1965).

3. Robert J. Sternberg, *Introduction to Psychology* (New York: Harcourt Brace College Publishers, 1997), 35.

4. Shaping is a term used by behaviorists whereby an animal, say a pigeon, is reinforced with food for behaving in a way which approximates the desired behavior. Through a series of such reinforcements the final behavior is achieved. (What better example of design in natural affairs?)

5. B. F. Skinner, *About Behaviorism* (New York: Alfred A. Knopf, 1974).

6. Joseph Rychlak, *Artificial Intelligence and Human Reason* (New York: Columbia University Press, 1991), 114.

7.   Ibid., 122–123, Quote is from D. R. Hofstadter, *Godel, Escher, Bach: An Eternal Golden Braid* (New York: Vintage Books, 1980), 709.

8.   Ibid., quote from Hofstadter, 713.

9.   Ibid., 123.

10. William James, *Psychology: The Briefer Course* (New York: Harper and Row, 1961), 62–63. Originally published by Henry Holt and Company in 1892.

11. B. R. Hergenhahn, *Introduction to the History of Psychology* (Pacific Grove, Calif.: Brooks/Cole, 1997).

12. Ibid., 243.

13. Ibid., 318.

14. Robert I. Watson, Sr., *The Great Psychologists* (New York: J. B. Lippincott Co., 1978), 403.

15. Michael D. Lemonick, "It's a Miracle," *Time*, 1 December 1997, 34–42.

16. B. F. Skinner, *Beyond Freedom and Dignity* (New York: Alfred A. Knopf, 1976), 192.

17. The philosopher Gottfried Wilhelm von Leibniz, who died in 1716, conceived of the universe as an infinite number of living units possessing consciousness that he called monads. The Greek philosopher Epicurus, who lived three centuries before Christ, was an early "atomic" theorist who postulated free will based on the ability of those atoms that make up humans to move about freely.

18. Pythagoras, who lived 500 years before Christ, believed that reality could be best known in its mathematical relations, which can be understood in abstraction but never adequately reproduced in the real world. For the Pythagoreans, the world of mathematical truth defines reality, and the material world as we experience it is an inferior copy of ultimate truth which exists in the spiritual, non material order of things. Pythagorean philosophy had an important influence on Plato and later Christian thinkers, most notably St. Augustine.

19. Morton Wagman, *The Sciences of Cognition* (Westport, Conn.: Praeger, 1995) 4.

20. Ibid., 7.

21. Immanuel Kant, "Prolegomena to Any Future Metaphysics", quoted in Morton Wagman, *The Sciences of Cognition*, 19.

22. William James, *Psychology: The Briefer Course*, 324.

23. B. F. Skinner, *Beyond Freedom and Dignity*, 189.

24. Edward L. Thorndike, *Animal Intelligence* (New York: Macmillan Publishing Co., 1911), 244.

25. The Hawthorne Effect (taken from research done at the Hawthorne Plant of Western Electric in 1924) refers to the phenomenon that subjects in an experiment may behave differently simply because they have been asked to participate in a study and not as a result of any experimental variable. Experiments on the effects of illumination done at the Hawthorne Plant showed that subjects performed better even when illumination was reduced—hence the Hawthorne Effect. The Pygmalion Effect, named after the Greek myth, refers to the

phenomenon of self-fulfilling prophesy, whereby the subjects in an experiment may change their behavior in the direction of expected results not expressly revealed. (Pygmalion was a Cyprian king and sculptor who fell in love with Galatea, an image of his own carving, to which Venus gave life.) This effect had been observed in the classroom thirty years ago by Harvard psychologist Robert Rosenthal and was recently reported in the Monitor, the monthly newspaper of the American Psychological Association. "The study found that the teachers with high hopes can raise students' test scores as much as three points or about 30 percentiles." *APA Monitor*, November 1997, p. 10. Those interested in this phenomenon should see Robert Rosenthal and Lenore Jacobson, *Pygmalion in the Classroom: Teacher Expectations and Pupils' Intellectual Development* (New York: Holt, Rinehart and Winston, 1968).

26. Joseph W. Krutch, *The Measure of Man* (New York: Bobbs-Merrill, 1954), 32, quoted in Gordon W. Allport, *Becoming*, 2–3.

27. B. R. Hergenhahn, 91.

28. Kirk J. Schneider, "Toward a Science of the Heart," *American Psychologist* 53 (March 1998), 276–277.

29. Blaise Pascal, *Pensées*, trans. A. J. Krailsheimer (London: Penguin Books, 1966), 90.

30. Johann Friedrick Herbart believed that compatible ideas connected to each in consciousness and formed what he termed the *apperceptive mass*. Therefore the apperceptive mass consisted of all those compatible ideas that one is aware of at any point in time. Other ideas that fight for attention are rejected by the apperceptive mass and are repressed into the unconscious where they can connect to other repressed ideas and together force their way back into consciousness, thereby creating a new apperceptive mass. Ideas in this way struggle for attention in consciousness.

Herbart did not believe that psychology could be an empirical science because this would involve splitting the mind into parts that he felt was impossible since the mind is a whole functioning entity.

Herbart's far-reaching intellect has influenced many other thinkers, notably Sigmund Freud whose notions of repression and unconscious conflict borrow heavily from Herbart. Also, Herbart's wholistic conception of mind has influenced twentieth-century humanistic and existential psychology. His rejection of an empirical psychology is reflected by many postmodern thinkers today.

CHAPTER 4

Personal Motivation

The locus of the act is the person.

— Gordon W. Allport, *Becoming* (p. 57)

Sigmund Freud has had an impact on many important thinkers, including many psychologists; sometimes his impact was at a personal level, as was the case with Carl Jung and Gordon Allport.

Carl Jung worked closely with Freud for many years in the early formation of psychoanalysis as both an intellectual and psychotherapeutic system. Eventually, Jung began to question some of the basic tenets of Freud's theory—especially Freud's emphasis on sexual motivation. "These doubts became so intense that in 1912 the two stopped corresponding, and in 1914 they completely terminated their relationship."[1] Apparently, it was an embittered relationship from that point on.

Gordon Allport is ranked as one of America's foremost psychologists of the post-Freudian era. (Freud died in 1939, and Allport's major work *Personality: A Psychological Interpretation* was first published in 1937.) Allport taught at Harvard for many years and was a prolific researcher and writer. In his biography, he tells of his encounter with Freud which affected his view of Freud's work. The incident occurred while visiting his brother, who was on assignment in Vienna. In Allport's own words:

With callous forwardness characteristic of age twenty-two, I wrote to Freud announcing I was in Vienna and implied that no doubt he would be glad to make my acquaintance. I received a kind reply in his own handwriting inviting me to come to his office at a certain time. Soon after I had entered the famous red burlap room with pictures of dreams on the wall, he summoned me to his inner office. He did not speak to me but sat in expectant silence, for me to state my mission. I was not prepared for silence and had to think fast to find a suitable conversational gambit. I told him of an episode on the train car on my way to his office. A small boy about four years of age had displayed a conspicuous dirt phobia. He kept saying to his mother, 'I don't want to sit there. . . don't let that dirty man sit beside me.' To him everything was *schmutzig*. His mother was a well-starched *Hausfrau*, so dominant and purposive looking that I thought the cause and effect apparent.

When I finished my story Freud fixed his kindly therapeutic eyes upon me and said, 'And was that little boy you?' Flabbergasted and feeling a bit guilty, I contrived to change the subject. . . .

This experience taught me that depth psychology, for all its merits, may plunge too deep, and that psychologists would do well to give full recognition to manifest motives before probing the unconscious. Although I never regarded myself as anti-Freudian, I have been critical of psychoanalytical excesses.[2]

Gordon Allport distinguished among three different types of personality traits: cardinal, central, and secondary traits.

In every personality there are traits of major significance and traits of minor significance. Occasionally some trait is so persuasive and so outstanding in a life that it deserves to be called the cardinal trait. It is so dominant that there are few activities that cannot be traced directly or indirectly to its influence. . . . No such trait can for long remain hidden; an individual is known by it and may even become famous for it. . .

It is an unusual personality that possesses one and only one eminent trait. Ordinarily it seems that the foci of personality (though not actually separate from one another) lie in a handful of distinguishable central traits. . . . Central traits are those usually mentioned in careful letters of recommendation, in rating scales when the rater stars the outstanding characteristics of the individual, or in brief verbal descriptions of a person.

One may speak on a still less important level, of secondary traits, less conspicuous, less generalized, less consistent, and less often called into play than central traits. They are aroused by a narrower range of equivalent stimuli and they issue into a narrower range of equivalent responses. Being so circumscribed they may escape the notice of all but close acquaintances.[3]

Allport's ideas paved the way for five decades of research on personality trait theory, which has proved productive as far as trait theory goes. Researchers have looked at studies accumulated over the years, including the work of such outstanding people as Raymond Cattell and Hans Eysenck, and have narrowed trait theory down to five universal traits known as the "Big Five." They are (E) extraversion, (N) neuroticism, (O) openness to experience, (A) agreeableness and (C) conscientiousness.[4]

Although trait theory has been a key area of investigation for many prominent researchers over the years, despite Allport's contention, it is of minimal value in understanding the person as a motivated human being. For example, a manager may realize that he is disagreeable much of the time in dealing with employees and may decide to change his ways. So motivated he is now able to improve his working relationships. Let's face it: a scientist, top athlete or a nun can all have similar personality traits but be motivated in very different directions. For all we know, Teddy Roosevelt and Humphrey Bogart may have had similar personality traits, but so what.

We should think of personality not in terms of traits but rather as a complex organization of different motivations. When we understand what motivates a person, we know something meaningful about that person, and therefore, the person becomes understood through an analysis of motivational dynamics.

Traits also have no moral dimension, whereas motives do. One's character is expressed in motives, not traits. Motives really exist, as does moral conduct, and biologists are now beginning to investigate the relationship between genes and morality. Richard Alexander has written a book that he has titled *The Biology of Moral Systems*. He writes: "I think I have shown that evolved human nature and morality are compatible, that morality as generally conceived, and possibly even as seen by idealists from philosophy and theology, is neither contrary to biologists' understanding of evolution by natural selection (as thought by T. H. Huxley, 1896) nor independent of selection, requiring a divine origin (as thought by Lack, 1957, 1965)."[5]

It is a short step from "moral systems" to "motivational systems," which suggests a possible biological basis for some human motives, especially at the *formative level*.

MOTIVATION SUPERSEDES PERSONALITY

Personality dynamics can be thought of as an internal patterning of individual motives. Motives do not stem from personality; it is quite the opposite. It is the cumulation and patterning of motives over time that make up what we call personality. In this sense we can think of the self as emerging from the motivational process.

A good friend comes to know the autonomous person within you, your values, your ideals, your interests, your needs, your aspirations, and so on. The you known is the motivated you—the you perhaps best revealed in quiet conversation. As suggested by Carl Rogers, human relationships are built on a congruence within the self between experience, self-awareness, and the communication of that experience and awareness.[6] Relationships build when selves are disclosed accurately to each other; when we share with one another our needs, interests, and values; in short, what motivates us.

Gordon Allport has proposed three levels of traits—cardinal, central, and secondary—to characterize human personality. Here is proposed a more dynamic model of the person based not on static concepts such as traits, but on a labile, interdependent, and shifting pattern of human motives—a system consistent with what Allport in his later writings refers to as a "person system." Here is developed more fully what was mentioned briefly in Chapter One—that the person is perhaps best understood in terms of a systems approach, whereby what we call human "personality" really consists of three autonomous and interdependent motivational systems. We will see how this relates to Allport's idea of a "person system."

A TRIARCHIC THEORY OF HUMAN MOTIVATION

These arguments were formed largely on the author's more recent work in organizational psychology, especially the theoretical and practical application of systems theory. In attempting to understand how organizations function, psychologists have turned to systems theory, which permits a conceptual model for an ever-changing process. The advantage of systems theory is its inherently dynamic and energetic character, which allows both consistency and flexibility. Systems theory is a very useful way of understanding how any organization can be the same yet changing at any given point in time.[7] This is also true of the human body. It is the same yet changing from moment to moment; and this constancy and variability are accounted for very neatly by thinking of the human organism as a composite of autonomous yet highly interactive and interdependent subsystems (circulatory, digestive, nervous system, etc.). If such a model is useful for understanding the functioning of the human body and the functioning of organizations, why not the human personality? Therefore the *triarchic theory of motivation* proposed in this book comes directly from systems theory which provides, I believe, a useful rationale for how people function.

According to general systems theory, there are several levels of systems ranging from those that are relatively simple and static to the most complex forms of human and social systems.[8] The higher the level of system the more open it is to outside influences. One way, therefore, of understanding a system is in terms of its degree of openness. A closed system is impermeable to outside forces whereas an open system is highly influenced by external conditions.

This triarchic theory of human functioning calls for a modified open systems approach in which three motivational subsystems are seen as autonomous, interactive and highly interdependent.

Figure 1

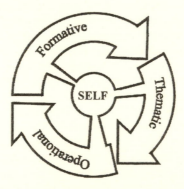

Triarchic Motivation as Interdependent Systems: Formative, Operational and Thematic

As portrayed in Figure 1, the motivational systems are: (1) the *Formative Motivational System,* which consists of *all* developmental experience bearing upon the present state of the organism, (2) the *Operational Motivational System,* which includes all current awareness, evaluations, judgments, and decisions; and (3) the *Thematic Motivational System,* which includes the directional activity of the person in terms of life's purpose, goals, and ultimate values in living. All systems are open in the sense that they are constantly being influenced by experience and new learning to lesser or greater degrees. All systems are interactive in that there is a continuing feed-in, feed-through, and feedback processing of data among the three systems. Also, all the systems are interdependent inasmuch as a shift in one system invariably affects the others and ultimately the total functioning of the person. Systems theory therefore permits a holistic conception of the person.

To be sure, many researchers have updated Allport's idea of a person-system since he originally proposed it forty years ago. David Winter in his 1996 text *Personality, Analysis and Interpretation of Lives* refers to two motivational systems, which closely parallel what can be described as the formative and operational systems. He writes:

While. . . conscious goals . . .are somewhat related to the less conscious, more long term and diffuse motives of Freudian theory. . . they are not at all the same. Our motives may be expressed in certain life tasks or personal projects [*operational system*], but such connections are not likely to be very close, because a broad motive such as achievement, affiliation or power [*formative system*] can be expressed and satisfied in a variety of quite different actions or projects.[9]

Winter, therefore, sees these motives as relatively autonomous, yet as systems, they are interdependent nonetheless. "Somewhat related" is Winter's way of expressing it. He then refers to the work of J. Weinberger and D. C. McClelland who "have tried to formalize the distinctions between these two motivational systems."[10] Winter continues: "In Freud's terms, this motivational system [*formative system*] is built upon the original motive reservoir of the id, for Rogers, it is part of our organism. In any case, as a part of our biological heritage, this emotion-driven system is sluggish and difficult to change. . . . Consciously formulated goals [*operational system*], on the other hand, develop with the mastery of words and language required for conceptualizing and expressing them. . . ."[11]

Winter does not develop the idea of thematic motivation as a third system. However, there is more than ample reference to such a system in the works of many holistic psychologists such as Allport, Rogers, Maslow, May, Frankl, Bettelheim and many others. The following quote from Frankl is representative.

Man's search for meaning is the primary motivation of his life and not a "secondary rationalization" of instinctual drives. This meaning is unique and specific in that it must and can be fulfilled by him alone; only then does it achieve a significance which will satisfy his own *will* to meaning. There are some authors who contend that meanings and values are "nothing but defense mechanisms, reaction formations and sublimations." But as for myself, I would not be willing to live merely for the sake of my "defense mechanisms," nor would I be ready to die for the sake of my "reaction formations." Man, however, is able to live and even to die for the sake of his ideals and values![12]

Here Frankl clearly distinguishes between *formative* defense mechanisms and the *thematic* ideals and values. Allport, May and others make a similar distinction.

Formative Motivation

Formative motives are those that provide color and quality to life. Although they can be formed at any time throughout one's life (e.g., learned behaviors, beliefs, attitudes, falling in love) they always are a prelude to current awareness. They also can be biologic in origin and can give life, not its purpose but its shape, its mood, its disposition. To use Winter's term, they are "emotion-driven." Unconscious motives as described within classical Freudian theory are formative motives, as are all other motives that contribute to the dispositional aspects of the individual, one's sense of zest, aggressiveness, elation, loneliness, depression, moodiness, and so on. Formative motives are loaded with feelings, attitudes, and habits rather than intentions. Feelings of guilt, remorse, anger and distress are the result of formative motives. So, too, are feelings of exhilaration, contentment, romantic love, vigor, and well being.

Formative motives are dispositional, including attitudes and habits, whereas thematic motives are directional. Thematic motives provide purpose, whereas formative motives provide mood. When you describe a person as "intense" or "happy-go-lucky" or "hopelessly in love," you are describing the formative motivational system. If you describe a person as committed to the cause of science and human betterment, you are describing the thematic self. The two are distinct. As there are volatile scientists, there are cool and collected killers. Although there is an important interdependence between the two motivational systems, they are essentially distinct and play very different roles in the development of the person. Allport's observation is interesting in this regard: "The first thing an adequate psychology of growth should do is to draw a distinction between what are matters of *importance* to the individual and what are, as Whitehead would say, merely matters of *fact* to him; that is, between what he feels to be vital and central in becoming and what belongs to the periphery of his being."[13]

Operational Motivation

Operational motives are those you act upon and live through, from day to day. They evoke conscious participation on the part of the individual. Each person is aware of operational motives, makes decisions and choices, and acts upon them.

Operational motives require conscious evaluation, planning and active decision making. Winter's term is " consciously formulated goals." When they are not clearly understood, an individual can be made more fully aware of operational motives by careful reflection, insight, advice given by a friend, or by counseling. The important feature of operational motives is that they can be consciously handled by the person. In part, they fall into the arena of cognitive psychology, which is concerned with the use of memory and in the thinking and judging process. The psychology of decision making and choice behavior also concern operational motivation.

Operational motives are those that are frequently clarified or come into focus by guidance or advice. The distinction between directive and nondirective approaches in counseling is frequently a matter of whether the motives are operational or not. Directive counseling and advice giving is most appropriate for operational motives.[14]

Operational motives also are "functionally autonomous" in Allport's sense. Examples may be as significant as choosing a particular career based on knowledge of interests and abilities or as mundane as whether to go fishing or wash the car on Saturday morning. We do many things in the course of our daily lives that have little connection to unconscious factors stemming back to early experiences growing up, and that have little relation to ultimate values or meaning in life.

Our decision to sleep in one morning could very well be motivated by what the party was like the night before, rather than any unconscious wish "to return to the security of the womb" because we felt rejected by someone at that same party. On the other hand, one's decision not to sleep in, but to get up as usual and jog two miles is likewise a current decision owing to the current waistline rather than old unconscious motivators. Life is full of operational motives for which we are fully responsible and accountable. If the boss asks for that report tomorrow but you had other plans for the evening, you are faced with a motivational conflict that is present and operational. What you decide to do—to stay home and work on the report or take your chances with the boss and go to the movies—is a function of present circumstances and an assessment of consequences. This is an example of operational motivation.

The famous social psychologist Kurt Lewin has developed a model for personal conflict that falls neatly into this discussion and can help in our understanding of operational motives.[15] Lewin describes three types of conflict: approach-approach, avoidance-avoidance, and approach-avoidance. In each case, the person is faced with a dilemma and must choose between two alternatives. Sometimes the alternatives are equally appealing, as with approach-approach conflict, or equally repugnant, as with avoidance-avoidance conflict, or the person must choose between courses of action that have both positive and negative consequences.

Examples are:
- *approach-approach*
  Go to the basketball game or have dinner at home with your family (both appealing to you)
- *avoidance-avoidance*
  Take a bus to Boston or drive (both displeasing)
- *approach-avoidance*

Stay home and write the report (displeasing) and impress the boss (pleasing), or go to the movies (pleasing) and fail at a chance to impress the boss (displeasing).

Much of life is concerned with resolving such conflicts, many of which are at the operational level. And so frequently, the dilemma and the potential consequences are temporary and peripheral and have no bearing on one's sense of personal meaning or purpose.

Freudians would argue that what appears to be an operational motive is in reality unconsciously determined and the decision is in fact predetermined by antecedent events that have caused the psyche to respond in one way or another. A Freudian might say that we decided on the movies because of an unconscious wish to fail—a fear of success. There is, of course, no way to refute the Freudian argument, nor would you want to, if you accept the deterministic premise of psychoanalysis. On the other hand, if one accepts decision making based on a current assessment of alternatives, then a distinction between formative and operational motives allows both possibilities to operate as probably they do.

Thematic Motivation

Thematic motivation consists of those motives that provide general direction in life. A thematic motive, as the word suggests, can be understood as the motivational theme that characterizes an individual's life. Such motives are persistent and enduring and highly resistant to change. They call for intense ego involvement and can supply the self with its esteem and sense of purpose. Thematic motives can be responsible for self-worth and an adult sense of identity; moreover, they are amenable to conscious awareness by self and others and in this sense resemble Gordon Allport's cardinal traits described earlier.

Because they provide life with purpose and direction thematic motives usually become crystallized in late adolescence or early adulthood. However, origins of thematic motives are likely seen in early childhood. (Examples are McClelland's achievement, power and affiliation needs.) Certainly, those people with whom one chose to identify as well as those who helped form our values play an important role in the formation of thematic motives, including possible conflicts among these motives. Thematic motives are more preconscious than conscious. They are, however, in their adult form functionally autonomous and therefore can be reflected upon.[16] Also, all functionally autonomous thematic motives can be changed through the efforts of conscious intervention and the human desire to change; however, since they form the basis for one's identity, this can be very difficult to do.

Thematic motives are best understood as themes for adult living. One of the principal responsibilities of the mature adult is to understand one's thematic motives and how such motives affect the course of one's living, one's satisfactions, one's frustrations, and one's sense of worth as a person—as well as how our thematic motives impact the lives of others. As Allport states, "The possession of long range goals, regarded as central to one's personal existence, distinguishes the human being from the animal, the adult from the child, and in many cases the healthy personality from the sick."[17]

There are three major thematic motives seen in adults: (1) ego-gratification, (2) self-actuation and (3) altruism. They are discussed at length in Chapter Five.

A LOOK AT THE THREE SYSTEMS

Since it is the viewpoint of this book that we can understand the person best in terms of motivation, it may be useful to compare the three types of motivational systems, developed above. Important distinctions exist among the three systems and each performs a different function in establishing an integrated personal life. All three are functioning in one form or another in each person, and each must be understood in forming a comprehensive view of the functioning individual. In technical jargon, formative, operational, and thematic motives in their various forms occupy the total variance of human motivation. All humans possess them in varying configurations. It is important also to stress that each motivational system operates autonomously yet interdependently with the others. In other words, there are three different and interacting motivational systems operating simultaneously in each person; at different times each system in turn may call upon more psychic energy than at other times, and there are differences for each person. To use Allport's term, they are "integumented" within the skin, but always open to new experiences.

Generally, individuals "feel" the activity of all systems going on at the same time. In the case of highly anxious individuals, the formative system draws upon more psychic energy than the operational or thematic systems. Such anxiety may make it very difficult to make decisions through the other systems. In fact, it is when the person begins to feel a sense of participation in the operational and thematic systems that one begins to sense a new freedom; that one begins to sense relief from debilitating anxiety and has the capacity to accept responsibility.

Thematic motivation, unlike formative and operational motivation, has an existential value in the sense that it concerns life's purpose, meaning, and values. It is through this system that we attempt to achieve existential meaning by actualizing our value system, moreover, the thematic motives are closely linked to one's sense of identity. Individuals who experience a life without purpose or meaning have inadequate or poorly constructed thematic motivation. It is in this general area of human travail that the existential psychotherapists perform their task. The existential psychotherapists are concerned with the thematic, and to a lesser extent, the operational motivational systems.

An important distinction, therefore, between thematic motivation and the formative and operational motivational systems lies in its existential quality. Formative motivation, which accounts for emotional tone and outlook, has no existential reference for the individual. Classical anxiety symptoms such as phobic disorders are not the same as experiencing a sense of loss in meaning. Since the '60s Rollo May and others have stated that the primary complaint of our time is a sense of emptiness—lack of sense of purpose, value, and personal power.[18]

It is the difference we find between the anxiety of, for example, an obsessive-compulsive individual and the existential anxiety, which, for May, is a lack of meaning. "In my judgment the best of the novels and dramas and paintings in our day are those that present to us the tremendous meaning in the fact of meaninglessness."[19] This loss of a sense of meaning or purpose is seen in even more devastating perspective during this postmodern period in which there seems to be even a loss of our sense of self. This is seen in destructive and reckless behavior, as well as in the media and various artistic productions. Littleton, Colorado is our most tragic example.

There is another very important difference between thematic and formative motives. Thematic motives, because of their emphasis on purpose, meaning, and values, are futuristic in character, whereas formative motives necessarily function out of the past, a past that is over and gone and never to be lived again. The question within the thematic motivational system is not: What has happened in the past to make me this way?, but: What do I want out of the rest of my life? If life is lacking in meaning and purpose, what can be done in the future to provide meaning and purpose? What decisions do I need to make? Where do we go from here? is the thematic question. What happened that brought me to this point? is the formative one. Thematic motivation sees human nature's most significant resource in its capacity for change, its power to grow and to adapt, the *elan vital* in us, as Henri Bergson once said. "'Creation...is not a mystery; we experience it in ourselves when we act freely,' when we consciously choose our actions and plot our lives. Our struggles and our sufferings, our ambitions and our defeats, our yearnings to be better and stronger than we are, are the voice and current of the *Elan Vital* in us, that vital surge which makes us grow and transforms this wanderer planet into a theatre of unending creation."[20]

MOTIVES AND THERAPY

This distinction also provides a rationale for the types of therapy that are most effective for different people. Since thematic motives are existential in quality and view the person's primary resource as the capacity for growth, methods of therapy that center on each person's inherent potential to grow and to actualize the self are most effective in dealing with this system. An individual's complaint of a sense of emptiness and a lack of meaning in living can be defined in thematic terms and therefore person-centered approaches that are existentially oriented are most effective in these instances. The philosophies and methods of Carl Rogers' person-centered therapy and Viktor Frankl's logotherapy are two psychotherapies that center on the thematic motivational system, in which purpose and meaning are critical.

Traditional psychoanalysis and other forms of "depth" therapies are primarily designed to deal with the formative motivational system. Psychodynamic therapy, as the name suggests, is oriented primarily to the past, the theory being that current psychological conditions are an inevitable consequence of experiences growing up. Psychoanalysis and other depth therapies see their purpose as deciphering those psychodynamics (formative motives) that produced the current emotional problem. As the key concept for such approaches is "insight," the key concept for existential therapies is "growth." The first centers on the therapist's ability to analyze the problem and to facilitate insight for the patient; the second centers on the patient's inherent potential for growth and development as a human being. The first is deterministic in philosophy; the second sees the person as essentially free and capable of change. Another distinction is that the first centers on the ability of the therapist, whereas the second centers on the capacity of the individual. This is more than a semantic difference, since the issue of belief in human potential is necessarily greater and more manifest in existential forms of therapy.

Thematic motives proceed from each individual's need for identity and meaning; for this reason, they are fundamental and enduring. Operational motives are not as closely tied to issues of identity and purpose, but they are nonetheless important, since they provide frequent opportunity for decision making and the exercise of free choice. Much of life's character and design are provided through operational motives. Education, career, and finances are often operationally motivated. Each person's ability in dealing with operational motives, however, is because of the successful working of the other systems. Since operational motives require active and free participation on the part of the individual, it is essential that the individual be capable of making effective decisions. This capability cannot be "forced." Within the formative system, certain individuals may be so depressed or obsessive that they are not able to make good decisions. In fact, since decisions create problems for such individuals, they may seek ways to avoid decision making. Likewise, within the thematic motivational system, the individual may feel so shallow or worthless that it is also impossible to develop the enthusiasm for creative decision making.

Cognitive forms of psychotherapy, as recently conceived, cut across the three motivational systems by confronting the individual with those belief systems that have interfered with a fair evaluation of the self in the world and distorted judgment and choice processes. Since importance is placed on learned beliefs and attitudes, there is a formative component to the cognitive approach; also, since cognitive therapy is concerned with readjusting one's view of reality in terms of reasoning and judging issues, an operational component is clearly manifest. More realistic perceptions of self in the world have direct impact on the release of personal values compatible with the real order of things—hence a potential thematic outcome. However, cognitive therapy in its emphasis on current awareness and problem solving does not strictly speaking, belong with existential forms of psychotherapy. It is primarily a form of psychotherapy that appeals to the operational motivation systems. Patterson and Watkins view it as a collaborative enterprise. "Collaborative empiricism seems best to characterize the therapeutic relationship. This means that therapist and patient collaborate in *testing out* the faulty thinking and conclusions that seem to so negatively affect the patient's current functioning. Conclusions become hypotheses—to be examined, studied, put to the acid test of reality."[21]

Another important distinction among psychotherapies is between nondirective and directive approaches to counseling. The nondirective approach claims that the client has the inherent capacity to achieve self-understanding and will seek solutions to difficulties congruent with felt and real needs through processes of growth and self-realization. The nondirective therapist creates an atmosphere of trust, understanding, and acceptance so the client can deal with uncertainties and ambiguities about self and others, and eventually work through to new degrees of self-realization. Such an approach is nondirective in that the client moves in the direction that is congruent with the emerging self. The therapist provides support and reassurance and becomes, as it were, a partner in the client's search for self-realization. There is a minimum of advice given. Personal goals come from the client, not from the therapist.

Directive counseling assumes a somewhat different view. The directive counselor believes that the client in seeking help relies upon the counselor as a resource, who by virtue of knowledge and experience can provide advice and counsel. Directive counselors feel that there is a place for giving advice based on their knowledge of personality dynamics and any new information gained while counseling, such as work history, academic record, or psychological test scores.

Directive counseling is an excellent approach in dealing with the operational motivational system. Decisions affecting marriage, education, career, and finances can frequently be assisted by advice provided by a competent counselor. A directive counselor may very well provide advice on academic and curriculum matters, type of school to attend, choice of career, family budgeting, and so on, since these issues are usually within the operational motivational system. Of course, the directive counselor must be confident that the client is able to utilize the advice given, and is not substituting a "career problem" for a more substantive problem that is within a different motivational system, and that may call for a different counseling method.

AN INTEGRATED STRUCTURE

We find that many psychotherapists choose to follow an eclectic approach, that is, to use the therapeutic method that seems warranted under the circumstances—also to vary approaches depending on the responsiveness and needs of the client. There is perhaps more wisdom in eclectic therapy than would first appear to be the case. Up to now, the eclectic argument went like this: "I don't worry about theory; it's what works that counts." The eclectic psychotherapist is pragmatic, choosing whatever method will produce results, and resisting being tied to any particular psychotherapeutic approach. For years, the eclectic psychotherapeutic argument was predicated on good therapy, not on good theory. This, however, has resulted in a lot of confusion and debate regarding the merits of eclectic forms of psychotherapy, since there is no adequate theoretical structure, and therapists shift from theoretical framework to theoretical framework without any integrating rationale. As Edward J. Murray has commented, "True integration requires a coherent theoretical structure which does not exist. We are still waiting for our theoretical integrator. In the meantime the best we can do is live in a state of irony and behave pragmatically."[22]

This theoretical structure may now be available. The current thesis, which distinguishes among formative, operational, and thematic motivational systems, now calls for an eclectic approach to psychotherapy and counseling since different methods can be more effective with problems within different motivational systems. Cognitive forms of psychotherapy and directive counseling appeal to the operational motivational system. In other cases, a nondirective, person-centered approach may be indicated for a problem within the thematic motivational system, and possibly a psychodynamic approach or behavior modification may be more appropriate for problems within the formative system.

TESTING

A word about psychological testing may be appropriate at this point. There are many different kinds of tests that use different techniques for soliciting responses from test takers, responses that are really small samples of a broader behavior pattern.[23] There are tests of human capacities and abilities such as intelligence tests, reading tests, tests of spatial relations, and so on. Such tests produce scores that can provide information regarding both the developmental processes and the quality of the environment. The formative motivational system plays an important part in these test scores, since developmental factors contribute heavily to an individual's problem solving and reasoning ability. A skilled psychologist, in administering the Wechsler Adult Intelligence Scale, can learn a great deal about the subject's emotional development from the manner in which the subject approaches problem solutions, the types of problems handled, and the skill in arriving at solutions.[24] The WAIS-R (revised), therefore, measures intelligence and provides an IQ score, but it also provides a lot more information to the clinically trained psychologist. Such data can be attributed largely to prior learning and to the activity of the formative motivational system. Various kinds of reading and learning disabilities have similar developmental origins.

There are also tests that measure interests useful in guiding the academic program of the student or in vocational counseling. Interest test scores as produced by the famous Strong Interest Inventory can be extremely useful in establishing career goals. Such tests tap the operational motivation system and those conscious processes involved in expressing likes and dislikes. Although it is true that the origins of some interests may be buried in the past, it is also true that many interests become functionally autonomous based on direct experience. Why, for example, should one look for unconscious motives underlying an interest in the outdoors when being outdoors is simply enjoyable in itself?

Other tests fall in the general category of "personality tests" such as the famous Minnesota Multiphasic Personality Inventory (MMPI) or the Myers-Briggs Type Indicator (MBTI). In most cases, such tests, notably the MMPI, seek information tied to the formative motivational system. Scores on the MMPI reveal such human qualities as hypochondriases, depression, and paranoia. Such terms are labels for formative motivational processes that characterize the individual's unique psychological structure. It should be noted that the MMPI, first published in 1943, was designed to detect psychopathology and was, in fact, validated using samples of psychiatric patients. A revision, MMPI-2, was published in 1989.

The Myers-Briggs Type Indicator is a widely used test that measures personality types stemming from the ideas of Carl Jung, Freud's erstwhile friend. (According to Larin Letendre, CEO of Consulting Psychologists Press, it is estimated that more than thirty million people representing fourteen different languages have taken the MBTI in different nations throughout the world.) The MBTI describes the person who takes the test in terms of four different score-pairs which can be combined into sixteen different personality descriptions. Types are more holistic descriptors than traits. They are more pervasive and enduring and may even be more genetically based than traits (although certain traits especially those described as cardinal traits by Allport may be genetically based as well).

Projective psychological tests such as the Rorschach and the Thematic Apperception Test (TAT) claim to reveal unconscious motives and inner drives not readily accessible to the ego. The theory underlying projective tests is that the person, in producing a response to an amorphous stimulus, such as an ink blot, is necessarily projecting one's unconscious drives and motives into the response to the stimulus. The theory of projective testing goes far beyond the scope of this book, but for those interested in projective tests it can be said that the Rorschach test and the TAT are similar in that they are both sensitive to the formative motivational system.

A widely used test that taps the thematic motivational system is the Study of Values first developed in 1931 by Gordon Allport and Philip Vernon. Scores are provided for six values: theoretical, economic, aesthetic, social, political, and religious. It is based on the theoretical formulation of the German psychologist Eduard Spranger, who published his work *Types of Men* as early as 1928.[25]

VALUES VS. INTERESTS

Human values, the kind we establish as fundamental priorities in living, unlike interests are processed by the thematic motivational system. For some, such priority values are the accumulation of wealth, for others, power; for others, self-sacrifice. In each case the thematic motivational system is at play.

Interests are very different. One person may like to go to the movies or to a ball game and share this interest in the movie or the ball game with the person sitting next to her—but they may have very different values and goals in life that relate only partially, if at all, to their interests. The distinction between interests and values is their force and centrality in the wholeness and continuity of the person. Interests may persist over a lifetime, but they don't define the person in terms of who that person is to self and others. Values, however, do define the person to self and to others. Any one of our interests in art, music, or sports does not define us as the person we are—probably not even for many artists or athletes. Jackie Robinson's values defined him more as a person than his interest in stealing home did.

Interests are distinguished from values in that interests are operational and values are thematic. At this point, it may be useful to provide a distinction made by Carl Rogers. Rogers, referring to the earlier work of Charles Morris, distinguishes between two different kinds of values—operative and conceived.[26]   According to Rogers, operative values take the form of preferences, likes, and dislikes, which are temporary and negotiable. Conceived values, on the other hand, are those that become internalized by the person and therefore can be useful in forming priorities for living. According to Roger's distinction, operative values, as the name suggests, fall within the operational motivational system, whereas conceived values fall within the thematic motivational system.

DRUGS

Drug therapy has become monumentally important in providing mental health services and is often used conjointly with other forms of individual and group therapy. Public acceptance and demand for psychotropic drugs has become so great that pharmaceutical companies have launched extensive research programs to investigate the psychophysiology associated with feelings of well being and related capacities to handle stress, assume responsibilities, and enjoy family and community relationships. Drug therapy has made an indispensable contribution to mental health programs, but not without suitable concern for the excessive use of psychotropic drugs by all ages, This is especially true where there is insufficient cognizance of individual life issues such as the need to be loved, understood, and accepted, and where there are life values to be examined and formed. It has been found, for example, "that the vast majority of psychotropic drugs in this country are currently prescribed by non-psychiatric physicians, with minimal training in the detection and management of mental illness."[27]

Consistent with these developments, the American Psychological Association has been pursuing the question of prescription authority for psychologists since the mid-'80s. In 1990, the APA Council of Representatives passed a motion to establish an ad hoc Task Force on Psychopharmacology, and by 1996, the APA had adopted a model prescription bill and training curriculum. "By the beginning of 1998, prescription privileges legislation was either pending or about to be introduced in seven states: California, Florida, Georgia, Hawaii, Louisiana, Missouri and Tennessee with five others actively planning for the near future."[28] The psychiatric profession is opposed to such legislation on the claim that prescribing psychotropic medications is the sole prerogative of the medical profession, and allowing psychologists without medical training to prescribe drugs would represent a "mental health hazard."

Up to now there has been a useful division between those mental health practitioners who were medically oriented and those who were psychologically oriented. (The old distinction was between "organic" and "functional" approaches to psychotherapy.) Pills certainly have their place, but so does the time-consuming art of listening attentively and speaking softly and supportively. There is no pill for empathy, understanding, and compassion, and no other way to build relationships, families, and society.

Psychology has made an enormous impact on our social mores and value structure, as well as our sense of self-worth and human capacity where sensitivity, understanding and good advice have been crucially important. Conversely, the medical profession, by making diagnoses for and treating of people seeking mental health therapy, has had an incredible social impact as well. Separateness has been a value, and we have learned from each other. It is hoped that as clinical psychologists become qualified to administer drugs they won't gradually surrender their traditional values and preferences for interpersonal therapeutic methods. The increasing demands of time and economic factors can reduce the clinical psychologist's commitment to time-honored psychotherapeutic techniques. There will be less listening, less empathy and understanding, less advice giving, and less challenging where the person's operational and thematic motives are at play. Psychotropic drug therapy is, after all, formative in its consequences since drugs work directly on the central nervous system and the endocrine system, primarily through the pervasive effects of neurotransmitter secretions and their reuptake by billions of neurons in the brain.

Effective formative functioning is essential for a healthy and productive life, but formative motivation cannot define life nor provide the goals, purposes, and meaning that make life worthwhile. Life issues are operational, but more so thematic when seen in the meaningfulness of life itself. Drug therapy has its part to play, but much of the stuff called human experience is outside the reach of body chemistry and resides in the spirit, the *elan vital* of our beingness. If there is anything the postmodern period has taught us, it is that psychology should take to heart now more than ever its important role in the care of the human soul.

NOTES

1. Hergenhahn, 492 (see chap. 3, n. 11).

2. Gordon W. Allport, "Gordon W. Allport," ed. Edwin G. Boring and Gardner Lindzey, *A History of Psychology in Autobiography* vol. 5 (New York: Appleton-Century-Crofts, 1967), 7–8.

3. Gordon W. Allport, *Personality: A Psychological Interpretation*, 337–338 (see chap. 2, n. 23).

4. Raymond Cattell in the United States and Hans Eysenck in England have done exhaustive research in personality trait theory. Cattell distinguishes between surface traits and source traits. Eysenck has constructed a three-dimensional model of personality traits. Many other researchers have been responsible for the identification of the "Big Five" traits, and over the years, different terms have been used. The five listed here are based on the work of Robert R. McCrae and Paul T. Costa Jr. See McAdams, 248–300.

5. Richard D. Alexander, *The Biology of Moral Systems* (Hawthorne, N.Y.: Aldine de Gruyter, 1987), xv.

6. Carl Rogers, *On Becoming a Person* (Boston: Houghton Mifflin, 1961), 338–346.

7. Fremont E. Kast and James E. Rosenzweig have conceived of organizational functioning in terms of six subsystems:

1) interaction with the broader environment
2) goal oriented
3) technical subsystem
4) structural subsystem
5) psychosocial subsystem
6) managerial subsystem

This system approach to understanding organizational functioning is developed in their text: Fremont E. Kast and James E. Rosenzweig, *Organizations and Management: A Systems Approach* (New York: McGraw Hill, 1974).

8. L. Von Bertalanffy, *Organismic Psychology and Systems Theory* (Worcester, Mass.: Clark University Press, 1968).

9. David G. Winter, *Personality, Analysis and Interpretation of Lives* (New York: McGraw-Hill, 1996), 354.

10. Ibid., 354. Winter makes reference to the work of J. Weinberger and D. C. McClelland in *Handbook of Motivation and Cognition*, E. T. Higgins and R. M. Sorrentino, ed. vol. 2 (New York: Guilford Press, 1990), 562–597.

11. Ibid., 354.

12. Viktor E. Frankl, *Man's Search for Meaning* (New York: Washington Square Press, 1984), 121.

13. Allport, *Becoming*, 39 (see chap. 2, n. 16).

14. Counseling psychologists make a distinction between directive and nondirective styles of counseling. Directive counseling calls for the counselor to be quite active and even to suggest solutions and recommend courses of action to the client. Nondirective counseling as proposed by Carl Rogers has an opposite view, in which the counselor is trained to be a sensitive and perceptive listener and thereby facilitate subjective solutions to problems without the need of advice or suggestions.

15. Kurt Lewin, "Collected Writings" in *Field Theory in Social Science: Selected Theoretical Papers* ed. D. Cartwright (New York: Harper, 1951).

16. According to Freud, the preconscious mind contains material that can be recalled "at will." The conscious mind can utilize preconscious material when it desires—not so with unconscious material, which by definition is unconscious and not available to consciousness.

17. Allport, *Becoming*, 51.

18. Rollo May, *Love and Will* (see chap. 1, n. 14).

19. Ibid., 110.

20. Will Durant, *The Story of Philosophy* (New York: Time Incorporated, 1962), 429–430. Quote is from Henri Bergson, *Creative Evolution* (New York, 1911), 248.

21. Cecil H. Patterson and C. Edward Watkins Jr., *Theories of Psychotherapy* (New York: Harper Collins College Publishers, 1996), 233.

22. Edward J. Murray, "Possibilities and Promises of Eclecticism," in *Handbook of Eclectic Psychotherapy*, ed. John C. Norcross (New York: Brunner/Magel, 1986), 413.

23. The reader may consult with any of several excellent books available on psychological testing. Anne Anastasi, a foremost authority in the field, defines a

psychological test as "an objective and standardized measure of a sample of behavior" as found in her text *Psychological Testing* (New York: Macmillan Publishing Co., 1982), 22.

24. *The Wechsler Adult Intelligence Scale* (WAIS), developed by the psychologist David Wechsler, is based on his original Wechsler-Bellevue Intelligence Test. It is always administered by a trained psychologist to an individual and consists of eleven subtest scores that when combined, produce a Full Scale IQ. It is an extremely popular and a widely used intelligence test.

25. Eduard Spranger, *Types of Men*, trans. Paul J. W. Pigors (Halle: Max Niemeyer Verlag, 1928; New York: Hafner Publishing Co.).

26. Carl R. Rogers, "Toward a Modern Approach to Values: The Valuing Process in the Mature Person," in *Readings in Values Clarification*, ed. Howard Kirschenbaum and Sidney B. Simon (Minneapolis: Winston Press, 1973), 75–91.

27. Ronald E. Fox and Morgan T. Sammons, "A History of Prescription Privileges" *American Psychological Association Monitor* 29 (September 1998), 42.

28. Ibid., 43.

CHAPTER 5

Three Ways to Go

> The most comprehensive units in personality are broad intentional dispositions, future pointed.
>
> —Gordon W. Allport, *Becoming* (p. 92).

Nicknames are special because they mean that others notice a uniqueness in a person that prompts a new name. But like all labels, nicknames have a strength and a weakness. Their strength lies in their specialness, their affection, and personalized humor. Their weakness lies in their distorted meaning outside of the close relations that invented the name. The label can become distorted when the unique meaning of its origination is no longer present. And so it is with all labeling systems. They run the risk of being distorted in meaning and creating misinformation. Outside of the originating microculture, they have no meaning—or worse, faulty meaning. Why Dwight became Ike Eisenhower and Alfred, Fritz Cavalier, is somehow lost in the personal histories of both men, and even when history can recall the circumstance, what was going on in the mind of the originators is forever unknown. For example Carl Jung's description of *extraversion* and *introversion* has to be read in the original. General usage of these terms is inadequate in expressing Jung's insights. In ordinary usage, *extraversion* means to feel the personal need to be in contact with other people. The outgoing person who seeks social relations and is comfortable with others is regarded as extroverted. Introversion has an opposite meaning. The introverted person shies away from social situations and can become anxious in social settings especially when meeting people he or she has not met before. For Carl Jung, the terms have a deeper meaning aligned with psychoanalytical theory. Jung uses the expression *attitude types* in describing the terms as follows:

The attitude types . . . are distinguished by their attitude to the object. The introvert's attitude is an abstracting one; at bottom, he is always intent on withdrawing libido from the object, as though he had to prevent the object from gaining power over him. The extravert, on the contrary, has a positive relation to the object. He affirms its importance to such an extent that his subjective attitude is constantly related to and oriented by the object. The object can never have enough value for him, and its importance must always be increased.[1]

Since Jung's early work in this century, there have been several notable and important attempts by psychologists to construct labels to explain human behavior. Typological theories, as they are called, have a long history going back to ancient times and remaining with us today. A good example of ancient influence on contemporary thought is the theory proposed by the Greek physician Galen, who lived in the second century. Galen suggested that a person's temperament was the result of certain humors found in the body; these humors were identified by Hippocrates five hundred years earlier as representing four elements of the material world—earth, air, fire, and water. Earth was associated with black bile, air with yellow bile, fire with blood, and water with phlegm. Galen associated these four humors with different personal temperaments, so that phlegm produced the *phlegmatic person,* who is sluggish and unemotional, blood produced the *sanguine person,* who is cheerful and optimistic, yellow bile was associated with the *choleric* individual, who is quick-tempered and excitable, and black bile was associated with the *melancholic* individual, who is sad.[2] Remarkably, these four temperaments were used in this century by Hans Eysenk in his description of human personality.

Carl Jung in his insightful work on personality types distinguishes among six typologies combining extraverted and introverted attitude types. They are the extraverted thinking type, feeling type, and sensation type; and the introverted thinking type, feeling type and sensation type. These six types represent primary functions within a person's personality. However,

For all the types met in practice, the rule holds good that besides the conscious, primary function there is a relatively unconscious auxiliary function which is in every respect different from the nature of the primary function. The resulting combinations present the familiar picture of, for instance, practical thinking allied with sensation, speculative thinking forging ahead with intuition, artistic intuition selecting and presenting its images with the help of feeling-values, philosophical intuition systematizing its vision into comprehensible thought by means of a powerful intellect and so on.[3]

The Myers-Briggs Type Indicator discussed in Chapter Four is based on Jung's typology.

OTHER IMPORTANT TYPOLOGIES

It was seventy years ago that Eduard Spranger's famous work, *Types of Men*, mentioned in the previous chapter, first appeared. In it Spranger offers a brilliant conceptualization of human nature in which humanity is viewed in a cultural context. In his words, "It is our intention to found a *geisteswissenschftliche* psychology of individuality, and ethnology or characterology."[4] Accordingly, Spranger characterizes humanity in terms of six ideal types: theoretic, economic, aesthetic, social, political, and religious. This portrayal continues to be used as the six human values measured by the Allport-Vernon-Lindsey Study of Values also mentioned in Chapter Four.[5]

The dominant interest of the *theoretical* person is the "discovery of truth." For such a person, it is most important to be a good observer of reality and to apply logic. They are always intellectualists, frequently scientists or philosophers. Their "chief aim in life is to order and systematize knowledge." The *economic* person is characteristically interested in what is useful. In one's personal life, the economic person is likely to confuse luxury with beauty. In one's relations with people, one is "more likely to be interested in surpassing them in wealth than in dominating them or in serving them." The *aesthetic* person sees his highest value in form and harmony. Such an individual need not be an artist nor an effete; one is aesthetic if one "but finds his chief interests in the artistic episodes of life." For the *social* type, the highest value is love of people in the altruistic or philanthropic sense. One prizes other people as ends, and is therefore kind, sympathetic, and unselfish. Spranger adds that "in its purest form the social interest is selfless and tends to approach very closely to the religious attitude." The *political* person is interested primarily in power. For such people, "a direct expression of this motive is uppermost, who wish above all else for personal power, influence, and renown." Finally, there is the *religious* person whose highest value may be called unity. Such individuals are mystical and seek to comprehend the cosmos as a whole, to relate themselves to its embracing totality. In many, "the negation and affirmation of life alternate to yield the greatest satisfaction."[6]

Spranger devotes a major portion of his book to a discussion of these "ideal types," but they are ideal concepts only, and most individuals would reflect a mixture of these types.

Later in 1956, Charles Morris's book *Varieties of Human Value* was published. In it, three dimensions of human value are explained. They are: dionysian, promethean and buddhistic. "The components were described as follows: 'the dionysian component is made up of the tendencies to release and indulge existing desires. . . . The promethean component of personality is the sum of. . . active tendencies to manipulate and remake the world. . . . The buddhistic component of personality comprises those tendencies in the self to regulate itself by holding in check its desires."[7] Again, as in Spranger's analysis, mixtures of these components are possible and Morris proposed six main combinations in terms of the relative strength of the component values. He also proposed a seventh combination in which all three components are moderately strong and approximately equal in strength. Based on this original analysis

Morris conducted extensive research that resulted in thirteen possible "ways to live."

A more recent attempt to classify behavior and one that has received considerable attention is John Holland's analysis, which grew out of his background as a vocational counselor and clinician. Holland proposes that most people can be categorized into six types: realistic, investigative, artistic, social, enterprising, and conventional.[8] He sees these types as useful in helping individuals achieve self-understanding especially for purposes of vocational choice and satisfaction. Holland's theory has been incorporated into a scoring system for the famous Strong Interest Inventory mentioned earlier. Holland has also incorporated his theory into a test called the Self-Directed Search.[9]

Jung, Spranger, Morris, and Holland have constructed systems for characterizing human personality that are essentially typologies. There have been other important typologies as well, such as William Sheldon's body type theory and Meyer Friedman's and Ray H. Rosenman's Type A and Type B, found to be associated with the risk of heart disease.[10] Typologies are logically useful but inherently limited for much the same reason that traits are limited. "Type" and "trait," whether genetically determined or acquired, are static terms. Motivation, on the other hand, is a dynamic concept.

This is a book about motives and motivation. Motivational systems are dynamic processes within the person that are revealed in a variety of ways. The three thematic motives developed in this chapter proceed from the self; they are in reciprocal relation to each other and interact with both the formative and operational systems. A motivational systems approach offers a model that is more dynamic and integrative than the traditional typologies of Jung, Spranger, Morris, Holland, and others. Indeed, Morris's original typologies, dionysian, promethean, and buddhistic, could themselves be prompted by different motives. Martin Luther King and Adolph Hitler both wanted to "remake the world," but for very different reasons and out of diametrically opposite motives.

THREE WAYS TO GO

Thematic motives provide life with direction, meaning, and purpose. The self has three ways to go—it can *indulge* itself (the gratification motive), it can *expand* itself (the actuation motive), or it can *expend* itself (the altruistic motive). Gratification motivation, actuation motivation, and altruism are the major enduring and pervasive motives within the thematic motivational system. (There are other thematic motives as well, such as loyalty to a cause outside ourselves, and honesty in all our relationships. They frequently are connected to one another and run through the three major motives in various ways.) We know that the thematic motivational system, as one of three motivational systems, has an extremely important part to play in the psychological development of the individual, especially adulthood when thematic motives are satisfied and begin to form an observable life pattern—a self-aware style of living. What is also most important is that thematic motives play a crucial role, not only for the individual and each person's sense of fulfillment in life, but also for society and the course of civilization. Obviously, whether humankind is given to processes of gratification, actuation, or altruism has tremendous implications for society and civilization. This point will be developed in Chapter Six.

As our lives follow certain themes, those motives that direct and guide our lives are thematic motives. In a very real sense, they are the most important motives of all, since they truly characterize an individual as having chosen a course, as seeking fulfillment, and as committed to a purpose. Mature people understand each other best and are drawn to each other most forcibly through thematic motivations.

When an individual lacks self-understanding it is frequently because of an ambiguity and uncertainty about the direction his life is taking. He may not understand his purpose for being or derive any real meaning in life. Such lack of purpose and meaning leaves an individual discouraged, aimless, lacking in self regard, without insight, desperate, and even hopeless. The psychologist Carl Rogers talks of the importance of direction in life. "The good life is a process, not a state of being. It is a direction, not a destination. The direction that constitutes the good life is that which is selected by the total organism, when there is psychological freedom to move in any direction."[11]

Direction is indeed important, and a person must feel good about the way one's life is going to experience "the good life" of which Rogers speaks. Indeed, the more committed and purposeful one's life, the better are one's chances. Even the individual who has known failure and disappointment can achieve "the good life" by adapting to a life direction wherein there is meaning and satisfaction. Some of our greatest figures have done just that. It is the basis for self-regard and, incidentally, is also the beginning of self-understanding. To know oneself, to be the kind of person who will choose this over that, who knows and enjoys the exercise of personal freedom, who experiences personal meaning in the private moments of life—this also is thematic motivation.

What is equally important about the thematic motives is that they provide such richness of meaning to human communication. They can represent a common bond against great odds or in spite of many personal differences. People of wholly different backgrounds, talents and abilities can be as one in a common purpose. Two athletes competing for victory are certainly more alike than differences in experience and personal philosophy would otherwise suggest. Thematic motives break down the usual differences seen in education and talent, yes, even in age and sex. Lovers are as one, and in this union of meaning, differences don't count. A couple dedicated to the growth and development of their children share a bond of dedication and commitment that unites them in a very special way despite differences in sex, age, and talents.

As mentioned many times in this book, we know each other best by our motives. Thematic motives are most revealing of the self, and as people grow in awareness of each others' thematic motives very little else needs to be said or known. We realize this when we love someone or we fear someone. When we dread someone or love someone it is because of thematic motivation in the self or in the other. Charismatic leaders are loved and feared for this reason. Charisma may be best understood as totally self-absorbing thematic motivation sometimes described as conviction or commitment. Since convictions appeal both to the mind and to the heart, they have enormous influence on us.

There probably are people who experience little thematic motivation—whose lives are really flat, lacking in color or character and just plain dull. Such people are usually crippled by overwhelming formative motivations. For such people, their growing up has depleted them of purpose and direction or has caused such severe anxiety that little remains to invest in living. As the saying goes, such people do not live, they exist. Typically, there is little if anything to know. They do not understand themselves or others because their apathy or their anxiety will not allow understanding of self or others to occur. They are the hopeless people of this world who have never won a good race. They are putting in time. Martin Seligman uses the term *learned helplessness* to describe people "whose learning experiences have hindered their capacity to grow and adapt."[12]

As one of the three motivational systems, the thematic system is autonomous and independent from the formative and operational systems. However, since the three systems are open-ended, they have a necessary interaction, so that when we speak of the whole person, we must take account of the three systems as making up the human personality. Individuals whose lives have force and direction are living thematically. For such people, the thematic system is in full swing, which means that such people have managed to exercise the freedom of their personhood and have a sense of willfulness, purposefulness, and ownership of their own lives. The thematic system is the most willful and the most consequential of all the systems. It concerns personal fulfillment and human destiny. It is permeated with the freely choosing self. It is sparked by freedom and personal commitment—the freedom Rogers talks of "to move in any direction." Without freedom and personal commitment, the thematic system fails to function and the human personality is characterized by either emptiness or flatness. Uninteresting, unexciting people and many "good time Charlies" have never known the exhilaration that comes with commitment. They are neither friend nor foe, hero nor villain, saint nor sinner. They exist in a world of uncertainty and fear, fantasy and withdrawal, and go blankly from day to day, from sitcom to sitcom, vacuous, unimportant and unhappy. There estimably are such people in our society where there is no tomorrow, only tonight's TV programs and the next trip to the mall.

The formative motivational system brings you forward to today, but as the saying goes, "Today is the first day of the rest of your life," which calls for a life of purpose and commitment. The human will, which has been inundated by technology and a Madison Avenue ethic, has to somehow revive itself, flex its muscles, and reach out beyond the media hype of these times. This is no easy task. Only those who make it happen begin to know the meaning in being alive. As Shakespeare said, "This above all: to thine own self be true."[13]

There is a difference between a choice and a decision. Animals may choose, but only humans decide. Skinner's pigeon may choose not to eat the food pellet because it is already stuffed—but this is not a decision. Humans decide on a way of life. Pigeons do not. Humans are capable of enduring hardships for a principle or an ideal. Pigeons are not. Humans can assassinate their heroes or forgive their enemies. Pigeons can do no such thing. To decide is to will; they are the same, and consequently, pure decisions are a completely human phenomena. To decide on a course of life may be the most difficult decision of all but inherently the most satisfying and potentially the most rewarding. Whether it is a decision for power or a decision for brotherhood, it is necessarily invested with the will. It is up to the individual to decide. "In the therapeutic relationship," Rogers writes, "some of the most compelling subjective experiences are those in which the client feels within himself the power of naked choice. He is *free*—to become himself or to hide behind a facade; to move forward or to retrogress; to behave in ways which are destructive of self and others, or in ways which are enhancing; quite literally free to live or die, in both the physiological and psychological meaning of those terms."[14]

All humans possess thematic motives but in varying degrees of intensity—from very weak to dominating in force. The stronger the thematic motive, the more it characterizes the personality. History provides many examples: a Lenin, a Mozart, a Gandhi.

Let us now look more closely at the nature of thematic motives. We have said that they assume a first order of importance in providing direction to human life. Within the thematic motivational system, the ego has three ways to go—it can indulge itself, expand itself, or expend itself. Clearly the ego can do many things with itself. It can protect itself, it can deceive itself, it can placate itself, and so on. However, these operations of the ego are not thematic. Ego defense, for example, is part of the formative motivational system. We speak of the defense mechanisms. From the thematic viewpoint, however, the ego is involved in self-indulgence, self-expansiveness, or self-surrender. Sometimes it will do all three; other times, one motive will predominate. For a lifetime, the ego can freely set its course in one of the above ways. The ego can indulge itself and seek opportunities for self-gratification; it can expand itself by engaging in activities that promote self-actuation; or the ego can expend itself, in pursuit of a cause or a purpose beyond itself. As Rogers has stated above, "it can behave in ways which are destructive of self and others, or in ways which are enhancing."

It is, of course, perfectly natural for humans at times to be concerned with their own gratifications. Pleasure is realistic and a natural part of each person's psychological and physiological development. Pleasure, moreover, is localized in the brain and has experimentally been shown to be a strong motivator.[15] Pleasure is natural and intrinsically desirable. A delicious dinner is more than a nutritious meal; it can be a delight to the senses as well. It is also perfectly natural for humans to concentrate on their personal development—to sharpen their abilities and talents. Both animals and humans enjoy stimulation at varying levels of intensity and complexity. Humans are forever curious; they have a need to explore the world around them. Feats of courage and endurance are most human indeed. Humanity's accomplishments against insurmountable odds, our motive to do, to succeed, to overcome, is one of our most laudable characteristics. There are too many examples to mention any one in particular but it can be safely said that human beings are universally interested in their personal development and in accomplishment. Science, art, and exploration are human and universal on earth and in space.

But is it natural for humans to love their fellow humans? Are we naturally concerned about the good of our fellows and of society? Philosophers and psychologists disagree on this point. Carl Rogers, like Jean Jacque Rousseau, would argue that man is essentially good. Rousseau used the expression *noble savage* to describe the person's primitive state unaffected by society. Others share the view that human beings are naturally aggressive. Thomas Hobbes felt that humans are inherently self-seeking and hostile creatures who require government to contain their destructive impulses. Freud's view on aggression is similar. "After long hesitancies and vacillations we have decided to assume the existence of only two basic instincts, *Eros* and the *destructive instinct*. . . . In the case of the destructive instincts we may suppose that its final aim is to lead what is living into an inorganic state. For this reason we call it the death instinct."[16] Conversely, there seems to be considerable evidence that we are not by nature aggressive as some would suggest, but that aggressive behavior is learned. Such a view has been expounded by social-learning theory, notably the work of Albert Bandura.[17] Nor are we completely given to libidinal drives and needs that make virtue a sublimation for a more base or primitive desire. Humans may be more loving than otherwise suspected. Harry Harlow's classic work on the "nature of love" based on research with macaque monkeys suggests a natural need for contact comfort, for love, and affection.[18] Even the archbehaviorist John B. Watson, founder of behaviorism, postulated that love was one of the three basic emotions of man. The other two are rage and fear.

Humans move toward each other, but such movement is frequently competing with other important attractions. It is for this reason that altruism may call for greater movement of the will than gratification or actuation. Self-surrender is not easy and, although arguably the most human of all motives, it is also always difficult to do; however, the fact that it is not easy does not make it less human or less joyful.

So it is natural for all of us to seek self-gratification, self-actuation, or altruism, and one or the other can predominate at different times; nonetheless, from a thematic point of view, only one of these motives can dominate over the long haul. At an operational level, any one motive can be more important from hour to hour or even from day to day, but at a thematic level, one of the three generally prevails. Humans choose not only what to do today, but they decide on a way to live. Deciding on a way to live—investing life with meaning and purpose—is thematic. One can not live by multiple themes. If one does decide thematically, a commitment is required. To live a life for self-gratification is different from self-actuation, which in turn, is different from altruism.

A fourth possibility is the person who is essentially without thematic motivation. This is the withdrawn apathetic person mentioned earlier. In this case, formative motivation could be so debilitating as to result in *learned helplessness*. There is little vitality and little hope. Such people find life to be empty and futile, lacking in meaning or purpose. They have no thematic motivational system to speak of. Generally, such people are dominated by the formative or operational system or both. They never achieve individual maturity and have limited capacity to achieve, to compete, or to love. As Seligman would suggest, they may have learned to be helpless. Such individuals either shrivel in the adult world or play the buffoon. Dominated by their pasts, they are determined by their upbringing, and their will is almost completely lacking. They have little, if any, ego strength and practically no sense of self. Their behavior is passive, infantile, neurotic, or psychotic. Extreme psychotic individuals are without will, do not operate coherently upon the environment, and have no purpose, meaning, or commitment. They are not even in the present—hence the psychosis. They are today in the past. They will never be born into tomorrow as long as they remain psychotic.

Then there is the individual without thematic motivation who is dominated by operational motivation. He or she is the dullard and the bore. Although perhaps "full of life," they don't know what life is all about. They mimic others and are constantly caught up in the latest fad, whether it be the latest fashions or taking the kids to McDonald's. They are led by the nose by Madison Avenue and *TV Guide*. Some may look "just great" but never feel quite so.

At this point, it is important to understand that people can actuate their full potential only through thematic motives. *Life is worth living at the thematic level, not below.* For this reason, it is impossible to enhance the human condition purely through behavioral techniques. To enrich human experience by treating the person at a formative level is also a limited approach. Psychoanalysis and behavior modification do not themselves enrich human experience. After all, people are proactive as well as retroactive. Man is concerned about destiny, meaning, and purpose. Although it is true that psychoanalysis and behavior modification may "free" the individual from restrictive dysfunctional behavior, they do not themselves educate the human to achieve a new congruence with others or with one's own personal meaning. The human character of courage, persistence, endurance, and dedication are never found in the formative or operational systems. The famous and the infamous are such by virtue of their thematic motives. Heroism is thematic as may be treason and treachery. Cowardice is not.

EGO GRATIFICATION

As mentioned earlier, ego gratification is one of three forms of thematic motivation. It is possessed by all normal humans and grows naturally out of early experience when the child's world is totally egocentric. As a thematic motive, however, the adult freely seeks opportunities for ego gratification. For some adults, such ego gratification is the dominant theme, and life becomes an incessant quest for more and more personal glory and gratification. The individual totally consumed with ego gratification has set a relentless course for power and pleasure, and the ego, fiercely committed to self-indulgence, seems never quite satisfied. It is never content. It knows no peace—just the relentless search for more power, more thrills, and more pleasure. Life is to live to its fullest, frequently at the expense of the less powerful and less fortunate. For such people, the only purpose in life is doing for one's self. To soak up as much pleasure and to achieve as much power as possible is the driving purpose of ego-gratified people. In their view, people who devote their lives to ideas, art, or care of others are fools; they are wasting their precious time by not living life to its full-est in the pursuit of pleasure and power. One need not be an Adolph Hitler or an Al Capone to be an ego-gratified person; sometimes very average people are marked by a cunning, a ruthlessness, or an inordinate need for pleasure that clearly characterizes them as ego-gratified people. There may be people in your organization or in your neighborhood who seek every opportunity for material gain and power without regard for the needs of others. They are devious, un-trustworthy, and self-seeking to the extreme. They see no point in honesty or in charity. For them, all intellectuals are "eggheads," all artists are "flakes," and all clergy are "stupid."

Ego gratification when taken to its extreme as a driving life theme, as a rea-son for existence, is both corrupting and corruptible. As such people contami-nate their own lives, they can contaminate the environment in which they live, especially when they serve as life models for younger people. For many, ego gratification can ultimately result in personal ruin and disaster. Here Hitler and Capone are good examples, but it is no less so for the person "next door" whose home is marked by frenzy and bitterness, where there exists constant discord and enmity, where jealousy and cruelty rule. For such people caught in the grip of ego gratification, a redirection of their lives by repeated acts of the will is the only dependable way out. Unfortunately, however, as this theme becomes more dominant, it is increasingly resistant to change, and a redirection of the will is much harder to accomplish.

It must be understood that ego gratification is true of all of us to some ex-tent. The question is not the presence of ego gratification but rather its domi-nance and its intensity. The human ego needs a certain degree of reassurance and recognition to function successfully. Abraham Maslow's theory of motiva-tion places ego esteem at the fourth (next to the highest) level in his hierarchy of motives. For Maslow, it is not until the individual achieves self-esteem in the form of a personal sense of competence and recognition for one's achievements that the person can move to self-actualization. So we should not regard ego gratification as something to be avoided. Quite to the contrary, for it is natural to enjoy a certain degree of praise and recognition. A pat on the back does us all good. The issue is one of degree and reeducation when ego gratification be-comes the be-all and end-all of existence. The Latin poet Horace gave us the following advice: "modus in rebus"—moderation in all things.

At this point, a more complete discussion of Maslow's theory may be in or-der. Abraham Maslow wrote an article called "A Theory of Human Motivation," which appeared in 1943 in *The Psychological Review*.[19] In it, Maslow proposed his famous needs hierarchy theory, which has been widely received until the pre-sent time. It is perhaps second only to Freud's classic theory of human motiva-tion, accounting for both lower level and higher level human need systems. Maslow proposed that human beings are constantly in a state of need emergence and fulfillment. In fact, he refers to the person as a "wanting animal." These needs exist in a hierarchy, beginning with the basic needs and going upward through the ego needs. According to his theory, there are five levels of need that are universal for all humans:

1) physiological,
2) safety,
3) love,
4) esteem, and
5) self-actualization.

All humans begin at a common physiological need level—the need for food, rest, water, and so on, which must be satisfied before the next order of need emerges. When the physiological needs are manageable and capable of satisfaction, the safety needs begin to emerge. Such needs are represented by safety from physical harm and a sense of personal security. This safety level is then followed by the love need, understood as a need for affection, intimacy, and belonging. Maslow regarded the love need when unfulfilled as a source of considerable unhappiness. It is not until the individual's love need is largely satisfied that the person then moves to the higher-order "ego needs." At the fourth-need level is the need for self-esteem, as experienced in a sense of achievement and personal competency as well as recognition by others. Finally, the highest-need level is the human need for self-actualization. In his original article Maslow describes self-actualization as:

the desire for self-fulfillment,. . . the tendency for him to become actualized in what he is potentially. This tendency might be phrased as the desire to become more and more what one is, to become everything that one is capable of becoming.
The specific form that these needs will take will of course vary greatly from person to person. In one individual it may take the form of the desire to be an ideal mother, in another it may be expressed athletically and in still another, it may be expressed in painting pictures or in inventions. It is not necessarily a creative urge although in people who have any capacities for creation it will take this form.
. . . .A musician must make music, an artist must paint, a poet must write if he is to be ultimately happy. What a man can be, he must be. This need we may call self-actualization.[20]

For Maslow, the individual is always in a relative state of need gratification and need emergence and is never entirely satisfied. As Maslow says, the human being is a "wanting animal" and constantly seeking new degrees of gratification and satisfaction. Maslow's theory, however, begins and ends in the self. It is essentially a self theory of human motivation in which the human becomes increasingly caught up with personal self-centered experience. Self-actualization is such experience in its highest form. Sorely absent in Maslow's theory is what can be called the *psychology of the other*, but more of this later.

SELF-ACTUATION

The use of the term *self-actuation* leans heavily on Maslow's and other theorists' concept of self-actualization. However, there is a difference in the meaning of the two terms. In this book, self-actuation refers to the need to utilize one's talents and abilities, to seek personal expression in creative and productive activities, whereas Maslow refers to self-actualization in existential terms, as the

highest level of one's beingness. The self-actuation motive is seen in many creative activities of an intellectual, aesthetic, or athletic nature, in an interest in
ideas for their own sake—art, music, and other forms of personal performance
characterized by originality and/or persistent effort. The writer, scientist, artist,
and performer are examples of those with self-actuation motivation. The individual whose life is dominated by such motivation is keenly interested in doing,
in creating, in utilizing one's talents. Such a person seeks personal expression,
he or she enjoys ideas, creative activity, excellence in sports, and so on—not
necessarily for any other reason but the sheer joy that comes through actuating
one's interests and abilities as a human being.

To use one's gifts, to exercise one's talents, all earmark the self-actuated
individual. The researcher, the sculptor, the composer, and the poet are such
people. But so are the explorer, the inventor, the trapeze artist, and the entrepreneur. Self-actuated people are known for their sense of urgency to do, to create,
to perform, to achieve a standard of excellence. They are not necessarily interested in power or fame for their own sake (although accomplishment may lead to
both), nor do they see their first purpose as assisting others. They just enjoy
doing, they love the search, the hunt, the quest of ideas and beauty. They are
both the dreamers in one sense and the doers in another sense. In a very real
way, they make the world turn. They are the Gallileos, the Newtons, the Shake-
speares, the Einsteins, the Mozarts; also the Magellans, the Nureyevs, and the
Babe Ruths of this world. They exist in history and they exist now, not only in
halls of fame but in your neighborhood. Any one of us may have this motivation
to some degree; some of us live our lives this way.

The exhilaration that comes with persistent effort and accomplishment is
one of life's greatest joys, and people who choose a life devoted to personal expression and personal enrichment are very fortunate. Such people can find great
pleasure working alone for long hours. Although they may enjoy sharing their
ideas and experiences with others, they somehow are always in their private
worlds; for the most part they think, plan and dream alone. They can become
extremely excited, even enchanted, by a new idea, a new notion or some reconfiguration of reality. There is something marvelous about the lives of such people who see marvels in life that others miss and who themselves create marvels.
But there is always the privacy, the loneliness and the solitariness that intellectually creative people typically experience. René Descartes knew this very well.
But so it is with many others who are self-actuated.

Of course, self-actuation carries with it a strong flavor of Maslow's theory.
According to Maslow, self-actualization is life's great experience, that rare occurrence achieved by so few people when somehow they gain a new sense of
awareness of their own being, becoming fully the kind of person they can be.
Such an experience really does exist, as it must have existed for Maslow himself, who does such a masterful job of describing it. Maslow, however, sees this
as the highest point man can reach. His hierarchical theory places self-
actualization at the very top, above self-esteem. Moreover, according to
Maslow, only a very few people (10 percent, perhaps) ever achieve a level of
self-actualization. For Maslow and others, self-actualization is the ultimate in

life. Yet the author disagrees with the leaders on this most important point. In this alternate view, life is not a hierarchy in Maslow's sense. Rather, living means moving from a life of reaction and preoccupation with the past and the present, to a life characterized by proaction, a concern for one's purpose and meaning. To live fully is to live to the future with commitment and dedication. The question is not one of level but rather one of direction. Thematic motives are invested with will, and it is the direction of willing that is all-important. A person who will never achieve a peak experience in the Maslow sense may nevertheless experience a life of meaning because of the direction of the will. He or she may live a life of love and struggle for others, perhaps family, parents, or children. Such a life is available to all of us and is, a more meaningful dimension of living than achieving self-actualization, which is limited to just a few people (10 percent). What is more significant is not self-actualization but self-transformation and going out of one's self—not an intensity of experience within the self (the peak experience, so called) but an extension of the self through active deciding into the life of others, *the psychology of the other*.

This brings us to the next thematic motive.

ALTRUISM—THE PSYCHOLOGY OF THE OTHER

Altruism is the pervasive motivational theme in the lives of many people, and fortunately, many of us have been touched in wonderful ways by this motive.

The altruistic person sees life in terms of the contribution that can be made for others; such an individual lives a life of service—a life frequently marked by self-sacrifice and patient effort in the cause of human betterment. Such people devote their time and energies in other-directed activities—in providing assistance to the needy members of society, the sick, the handicapped, and the poor, as well as others seeking care and attention; children and older people are an example. Altruistic people derive life's greatest satisfactions and are most fulfilled when they can somehow be of assistance to others in need of assistance. To such people, life was meant to live not for self but for others, and the true meaning of life can be found only in this giving relationship to other people.

The altruistic motive can be found in many forms at various levels of intensity. For some, the role of loving parent or child can fill this motive very nicely, whereas for others, it may take some vocational form such as teaching, medicine, or social work. In the case of Jackie Robinson, it took the form of baseball. It can be serene and unnoticed or bold and heroic, but always it is the result of human effort and will. It is a motive prompted not by curiosity, intellectuality, or creative urges, but simply, and often unobtrusively, by human intentionality and good will. Altruism can be a dominant life theme for the gentle and loving parent no less than for the martyr or missionary. It finds expression in many ways, ranging from the schoolteacher whose concern for his or her "children" is deep and meaningful, to the bank executive who devotes evenings and weekends managing a volunteer human service organization. The person who volunteers for Compeer or a similar human service organization is an excellent living example. Another living example is Jim Snow, a 1974 graduate of Regis High

School in New York City. The following was reported in the Summer 1998 issue of the Regis Alumni News:

James G. Snow '74 received the second annual John Francis Regis Award at the Alumni Senior Luncheon on May 4, 1998. The award is presented to an alumnus who fulfills the ideals which the patron saint of the school displayed during his life. . . .

    After practicing law for several years. . .[Jim] decided to forego a career in that profession. He chose instead to address the educational needs of deprived men, women and children in a life of service; to be a "man for others." . . .

In presenting the award Fr. J. Thomas McClain, S.J. added:

[Jim's] work has been in one form or other the work of education, thereby giving those in need an opportunity to get ahead through achieving a higher level of learning and skill. This has brought Jim in contact with the homeless, at-risk youth, Portuguese immigrants, those struggling with various forms of substance abuse, as well as those trying to reestablish themselves after being released from jail.

    Jim has worked with mothers losing custody of their children. . . . runaway teenagers. . . victims of sexual and physical abuse—the list goes on. In whatever struggle that the individual carried, Jim has worked tirelessly to give that person an opportunity to move ahead through the gift of education: so that they can qualify for a job and create stability in their lives.

    Jim Snow illustrates what can happen in anyone's life through the power of personal decision making. Snow made a tough personal decision and made it stick—to be a "man for others."[21] This is altruism plain and simple, a clear case of the *psychology of the other.*

    A film produced many years ago by the National Education Association featured Miss Sweet (real name), an elderly schoolteacher, who many years ago in a little town in Arizona had Ralph Bunche among her students. Bunche had since become a statesman of international rank—a personal force in the United Nations who in 1950 was the first black person to win the Nobel Peace Prize. The film portrayed Miss Sweet as the teacher who had the most profound impact upon him—a kindly lady and undoubtedly a good teacher, but probably much more than that. She was more than just a teacher; a giving human being whose life was invested with the will to serve and help others steadfastly and lovingly. In any event, Bunche, when asked to search through his remembrance for the teacher who meant the most to him, thought of a fine and simple lady whom he knew as a student many years before. Brought from a life of obscurity to national fame by the remembrance of her most famous student, Miss Sweet's life had been one of quiet yet forceful devotion to others. Martin Luther King and Mother Teresa are more dramatic, but perhaps no more heroic examples.

    Altruism is the expenditure of the self in the service of others. The point was made earlier that within the thematic motivational system, the ego has three ways to go: to indulge itself, to expand itself, and to expend itself. Altruism is the third way— the ego expending the efforts and resources of the person toward a goal or a cause beyond the person, beyond the self. It is for all of us. It is in this process of giving of the self that true actualization is realized most fully. It is the *psychology of the other*, not limited to a few, as in Maslow's description of the self-actualized person. It is in the movement of the will that each person's humanity is experienced most fully, for we know that it is in the act of willing that human beings best express their being and their uniqueness, contrary to what biologists tell us is the selfishness of our genetic makeup. We don't have to be self-actualized to be capable of this. Maslow in his later writings uses the *terms metamotivation* and *transcendence* as ways of describing the lofty heights of human nature, as if there were a kind of angelic component of human motivation that a few—not all, just a few—could realize. For example, Maslow speaks of "identification love" as a "kind of transcendence, e.g. for one's child, or for one's beloved friend . . . . It implies also a wider circle of identification, i.e. with more and more people approaching the limit of identification with all human beings."[22]

Sounds good, but how about the rest of us? How about the kid who gives up his spot on the starting team so the new kid in town can get to play? Maslow takes human nature to beautiful heights in his concept of metamotivation and transcendence, but he never comes out squarely in favor of all of us who try to be good guys. "Love thy neighbor as thyself" has been transposed into the verbiage of humanistic-existential psychology and has lost its gut meaning for all us. Duane Schultz, author of several popular texts in psychology, in his criticism of Carl Roger's view of personality states the case clearly and parallels this author's opinion of Maslow's concept of "the self."

The emphasis is on experiencing, feeling and living fully for oneself without a corresponding emphasis on love, dedication, or commitment to a cause, purpose, or person other than "me" and "my" fresh experience of each moment. This vision of the healthy personality lacks a sense of an active caring, responsible relationship to other persons or to society. The fully functioning person seems to be the center of the world, not an interacting, responsible participant in it. The concern is solely with one's own existence, not with fostering the growth and development of another.[23]

Schultz is clearly for a *psychology of the other*.

To choose to live one's life primarily out of a concern for others, whether humbly or grandiloquently, is certainly a most human kind of activity and one that none of us can afford to live without, whether as recipients or givers. One who does for others will someday do for us, too, since the effect of human goodness knows no bounds, not even the ultimate boundary of death itself. It is the thematic motive of altruism that has the greatest consequence—for only in loving does death achieve any meaning, a meaning not possible within the realms of the self alone but possible only when the self is infused with love and the will to love.

The altruistic motive is really the basis of life itself. Certainly, human life has no meaning without love and mutual regard. Love propels life, sustains it, shapes it, and can even provide meaning in death. It is hoped that we all are and will continue to be the continuing beneficiaries of altruistic motivation, as there really is no other way in which the human race will survive. As mentioned many times in this book, survival will depend not on human intelligence but on human will—a will that moves in the direction of concern for others and concern for our children. This the psychologist Erik Erikson calls *generativity*.[24] Other thematic motives are either too selfish or too egocentric to account for human survival. It is for this reason that altruism is so compatible with human freedom, since one cannot be altruistic unless freely choosing to be so, and one is less than altruistic if impinging on the freedom of others.

WHAT BIOLOGISTS THINK ABOUT ALTRUISM

Biologists generally support the conclusion that altruistic behavior is primarily self-serving and, as has been observed in other species, humans will display altruistic behavior to their near relatives first to preserve their own genes. Edward O. Wilson, the sociobiologist, calls altruistic behavior, when done without the expectation of personal reward, "hard-core" altruism. At the other end of the continuum, he sees "soft-core" altruism as essentially selfish.

"My own estimate of the relative proportions of hard-core and soft-core altruism in human behavior is optimistic. Human beings appear to be sufficiently selfish and calculating to be capable of indefinitely greater harmony and social homeostasis. This statement is not self-contradictory. True selfishness, if obedient to other constraints of mammalian biology, is the key to a more perfect social contract."[25]

He continues: "Individual behavior, including seemingly altruistic acts bestowed on tribe and nation, are directed, sometimes very circuitously, toward the Darwinian advantage of the solitary human being and his closest relatives. The most elaborate forms of social organization, despite their outward appearance, serve ultimately as the vehicles of individual welfare."[26]

Not everyone agrees. Christopher Boehm in an article in *Behavioral Science* expresses his difficulty with the sociobiological argument:

Most actual human behaviors which fit cultural definitions of altruistic selflessness may be assumed to involve much direct self-interest in terms of the real motivation which is operating. Saints, we may assume, are often bucking for the status of sainthood just as much as they are interested in helping others, motivationally speaking. War heroes are often driven more by desire for achievement, fear of the social status of cowardice, or self-doubt than a pure concern for the abstract altruistic principles which are voiced when they receive their medals. Obviously this motivational variability behind human behaviors codified as altruistic poses a very serious problem for one who wishes to assume a single set of genes prepares such self-sacrificial behavior, an assumption which prominent sociobiologists appear to make.[27]

Because he sees altruism in motivational terms, Boehm questions the nature of the linkage between genes and so called altruistic behavior. Richard Alexander has this to say:

I suspect that nearly all humans believe it is a normal part of the functioning of every human individual now and then to assist someone else in the realization of that person's own interests to the actual net expense of those of the altruists. What this "greatest intellectual revolution of the century" tells us is that, despite our intuitions, there is not a shred of evidence to support this view of beneficence, and a great deal of convincing theory suggests that any such view will eventually be judged false.[28]

Richard Dawkins, the popular author of many books on Darwinian evolution, has a more hopeful view of things. He concedes that human altruism should be taught and may in fact be heavily influenced by culture. He writes:

If you wish, as I do, to build a society in which individuals cooperate generously and unselfishly toward a common good, you can expect little help from biological nature. Let us try to teach generosity and altruism, because we are born selfish. Let us understand what our selfish genes are up to, because we may then at least have the chance to upset their designs, something which no other species has ever aspired to. . . .

Our genes may instruct us to be selfish, but we are not necessarily compelled to obey them all our lives. It may just be more difficult to learn altruism than it would be if we were genetically programmed to be altruistic. Among animals, man is uniquely dominated by culture, by influences learned and handed down. Some would say that culture is so important that genes, whether selfish or not, are virtually irrelevant to the understanding of human nature. Others would disagree. It all depends where you stand in the debate over 'nature versus nurture' as determinants of human attributes.[29]

From this statement it is safe to conclude that Dawkins, the world-famous evolutionist, is himself in favor of a *psychology of the other* and the personal responsibility this entails—which of course, Alexander's skepticism notwithstanding, puts us squarely into the motivational arena once again. Although altruism provides many opportunities for drama and heroism, such drama is less common than the simple heroics of everyday living. Whether at home, at work, or in the community, altruism builds trust and mutual understanding which is the basis for constructive effort toward a better society.

NOTES

1. Carl Jung, *The Portable Jung*, ed. Joseph Campbell, trans. R. F. C. Hull (New York: Viking Press, 1976), 178–179.

2. Hergenhahn, 34 (see chap. 3, n. 11).

3. Jung, 268.

4. Spranger, 104 (see chap. 4, n. 25).

5. Gordon W. Allport, Phillip E. Vernon, and Gardner Lindzey, *Study of Values: A Scale for Measuring Dominant Interests in Personality* (New York: Houghton-Mifflin 1970).

6. Ibid., 4–5.

7. Charles Morris, *Varieties of Human Value* (Chicago: University of Chicago Press, 1956), 2.

8. John L. Holland, *Making Vocational Choices* (Englewood Cliffs, N. J.: Prentice-Hall, 1973).

9. John Holland, *Professional Manual for the Self-Directed Search* (Palo Alto, Calif.: Consulting Psychologists Press, 1979).

10. William H. Sheldon proposed a theory whereby personality type was found to be associated with three different physical types: ectomorph (thin),

mesomorph (athletic) and endomorph (obese). For a discussion, see William H. Sheldon, *The Varieties of Temperament: A Psychology of Constitutional Differences* (New York: Harper and Brother, 1942). A discussion of Type A and Type B personalities can be found in Meyer Friedman and Ray H. Rosenman, "The Key Cause—Type A Behavior Pattern", in *Sources: Notable Selections in Psychology*, ed. Terry F. Pettijohn (Guilford, Conn.: Dushkin Publishing Group, 1994), 273–280.

11. Carl Rogers, *On Becoming a Person* (Boston: Houghton-Mifflin, 1961), 186.

12. Martin E. P. Seligman, "Depression" in *Sources: Notable Selections in Psychology* ed. Terry F. Pettijohn (Guilford, Conn.: Dushkin Publishing Group, 1994), 290–294.

13. *Hamlet* 1.3.82, William Shakespeare, *The Tragedy of Hamlet, Prince of Denmark*, eds. Tucker Brooke and Jack Randall Crawford (New Haven: Yale University Press, 1954).

14. Rogers, *On Becoming a Person*, 192 (see chap. 4, n. 6).

15. "In 1954, James Olds and Peter Milner discovered that electrical stimulation of certain parts of the brain could serve as reinforcement;. . . If it is arranged that an animal can press a bar that delivers electrical stimulation to the brain through permanently implanted electrodes the animal will press the bar frequently (up to 100 presses per minute)." R. L. Isaacson and Carol Van Harteveldt, "Neural Basis of Behavior" in *Foundations of Contemporary Psychology*, ed. Merle E. Meyer (New York: Oxford University Press, 1979), 126.

16. Sigmund Freud, "Outline of Psychoanalysis," (1940) quoted in Ernest R. Hilgard, *Psychology in America* (New York: Harcourt Brace Jovanovich, 1987), 370.

17. Albert Bandura, Dorothea Ross, and Sheila A. Ross, "Imitation of Film-Mediated Aggressive Models," *Journal of Abnormal and Social Psychology* 66 (1963), 3–11.

18. Harry Harlow performed an ingenious experiment in which baby macaque monkeys were placed in a cage with two surrogate mothers, one made of wire mesh and the other made of soft terry cloth—the wire "mother" providing food for one group of monkeys, and the cloth "mother" providing food for another group.

Harlow's results showed that regardless of how the monkeys were fed, they tended to spend most of their time with the cloth "mother," presumably because the monkeys preferred the softness and comfort of the terry cloth "mother." This occurred despite the fact that the hunger drive was satisfied for one group by the wire mesh "mother." Harry F. Harlow, "The Nature of Love," *American Psychologist*, 13 (1958), 673–685.

19. Abraham Maslow, "A Theory of Human Motivation," 382–383 (see chap. 1, n. 12).

20. Ibid., 381.

21. *Regis Alumni News* (New York) 63 (Summer 1998) 1, 13.

22. Abraham Maslow, *The Farther Reaches of Human Nature* (New York: Penguin Books, 1982), 262.

23. Duane Schultz, *Growth Psychology: Models of the Healthy Personality* (New York: D. Van Nostrand Co., 1977), 37.

24. Erik H. Erikson, *Insight and Responsibility* (New York: W. W. Norton & Co., 1964), 131.

25. Edward O. Wilson, *On Human Nature* (Cambridge: Harvard University Press, 1978), 157.

26. Ibid., 158-159.

27. Christopher Boehm, "Some Problems With Altruism in Search for Moral Universals," *Behavioral Science* 24 (January 1979), 15.

28. Alexander, 3 (see chap. 4, n. 5).

29. Richard Dawkins, *The Selfish Gene* (New York: Oxford University Press, 1976), 3.

CHAPTER 6

Setting a Course

There is properly no history, only biography,
—Ralph Waldo Emerson, *The Selected Writings of Ralph Waldo Emerson* (p. 116)

About thirty-five years ago, Stanley Milgram, a social psychologist at Yale, ran a series of studies that caused a lot of controversy among psychologists at that time, and that continues to be a topic of discussion today.[1] Milgrim contrived an experiment in which he allowed his participants to believe that they were inflicting electric shocks of increasing intensity on a person whenever the person failed to provide correct answers on a test of memory for paired words. No shocks were actually administered, but those who participated in the study did not know this. They were required by the experiment to increase the voltage every time there was a wrong answer given, and a majority did so, up to 450 volts. A dummy generator recorded the voltage from "Slight Shock" to "Danger: Severe Shock."[2]

This became one of the most famous (and infamous) experiments in all of psychology and is debated to this day for its results and for its method. Milgram was interested in investigating the extent to which individuals who were subject to the authority of another person would perform an act at odds with their own best judgment and inclination. Increasing the voltage was perceived by the participants in the study as causing great distress—even pain—for the person giving the wrong answers. The following quotation is taken directly from Milgram's research report.

The victim indicates no discomfort until the 75-volt shock is administered, at which time there is a light grunt in response to the punishment. Similar reactions follow the 90- and 105-volt shocks, and at 120 volts the victim shouts to the experimenter that the shocks are becoming painful. Painful groans are heard on administration of the 135-volt shock and at 150 volts the victim cries out, 'Experimenter get me out of here! I won't be in the experiment any more! I refuse to go on. . . .' and by 270 volts his response to the shock is definitely an agonized scream. . . . and at 315 volts, after a violent scream he reaffirms with vehemence that he is no longer a participant. From this point, he provides no answers, but shrieks in agony whenever a shock is administered; this continues through 450 volts. Of course, many subjects will have broken off before this point.[3]

But the overwhelming majority of participants persisted in applying increased voltage when the experimenter required that they do so. When voice feedback, as described above, was given, "sixty-two percent of the subjects obeyed the experimenter's demands fully."[4] Unfortunately, what we learned from this study had already been established from our knowledge of recent history. The acts performed by the Nazis during the Holocaust were far more heinous than the electric shocks in the Yale laboratory. In the face of estimates that six million Jews were systematically annihilated by Hitler and his executioners, a controlled study involving a handful of people in a well-equipped psychological laboratory on the Yale campus seems pitiful by comparison. Do we need psychological studies to demonstrate that blind allegiance to corrupt power exists? Are not historical accounts humiliating enough? Gang lynchings, hate crimes, and torture happen. The savage beating and murder of Matthew Shepard in Wyoming is one of many lurid examples. Do we have to investigate these phenomena in social psychological studies? Can we honestly believe that we have reconstructed the conditions of inhuman obedience to authority so well that comparative statements can be made? To what end? Also, by restructuring the problem in research jargon—by objectifying it in academic terms—do we somehow make it more remote and more easy to "understand"? Can such evil somehow be rationalized as induced by environmental forces? Can such evildoing be understood as some kind of socially conditioned response? People do wrong things, psychological theory notwithstanding.

There are many times when history supersedes science and provides more reliable information. The following story illustrates this point. Over the years the author has shown a film of the Milgram research to students in Introductory Psychology. It holds their attention, and usually produces good discussion for both its content and its method. However, after viewing it several times, one eventually realizes that Milgram himself was guilty of perpetrating the very act he was investigating. In the film, the participants are pressured by the researcher to continue to administer electric shocks up to 450 volts. Most do so, but the film shows several participants expressing considerable stress and becoming visibly upset at having to continue. "There were powerful reactions of tension and emotional strain in a substantial proportion of the participants. Persons were observed to sweat, tremble, stutter, bite their lips, and groan as they found themselves increasingly implicated in the experimental conflict."[5] Some participants stop the experiment and object strenuously when told they must persist. Some are adamant in their refusal, but most yield to the pressure of authority. This human conflict and turmoil is dramatically present in the experiment, but the focus is on the wrong participant. The true participant is the experimenter himself who is required by the research design to compel participants to experience personal anguish in yielding to the pressure he applies. The experimenter witnesses their distress, yet coldly enforces authority on the participants with unrelenting determination. The experimenter becomes the culprit by being personally responsible for the distress and anguish the participants visibly display when forced to continue to administer shocks against their best inclination. Scientific objectivity make the experimenter impervious to such human feelings as doubt, shame, regret, and remorse—or if these emotions are experienced, they are not investigated or reported by Milgram. Arthur Miller in his book, *The Obedience Experiments*, devoted entirely to Milgram's research, cites Rom Harré and Lewis Brandt as advancing a similar criticism. —"that Milgram was the 'authority' figure in a hierarchy—the research team".[6] Rom Harré writes:

One of the more remarkable features of the Milgram series of studies was the behavior of the assistants who, in carrying out the experiments, were obeying Milgram. . . . The most morally obnoxious feature of this outrageous experiment was, I believe, the failure of any of Milgram's assistants to protest against the treatment that they were meting out to the subjects. At least the citizens of Newhaven [*sic*] in the measure of one in three had a finer moral sensibility than any of those who assisted Milgram in this unpleasant affair.[7]

Brandt observes that "Had Milgram critically analysed his experimental procedure before carrying out his experiments, he would have (1) known the results beforehand (since he was willing to make his participants suffer in the name of science, his participants would do the same). . . ."[8]

Perhaps the truly important finding of Milgram's research is that under the guise of science, experimenters can become desensitized to the distress of others and inflict pain if the study requires they do so. We know, for example, that among the atrocities of the Holocaust were human experiments conducted by qualified medical doctors. There is a serious caveat in this hypothesis as we enter the next millennium and already observe, as in the case of proposed human cloning, science over humanity. What of the clone's sense of self, *its* sense of personhood, *its* humanity? In the final analysis, Milgrim is the instigator who perpetrates upon his colleagues those very actions his study is designed to reveal. It seems that little thought has been given to this fact and no mention made of it in his several reports. In the face of this, the research data are superseded by the "historical" fact of the experimenter's behavior, for which no experimental data is recorded. For this famous study, the historical account of what was done is more important than the data itself.

HITLER

Hitler is a special case in all of human history. He is the archcriminal of all time. Special not only for the enormity of his crimes but also for the perplexity and seductiveness of his personality, his ability to mesmerize with his look, his voice, and his gesture. Scholars—historians, psychohistorians, psychoanalysts, and journalists have grappled with this human enigma since he first rose to power in the early twenties.

His life and his deeds bring into stark contrast the difference in actions which are seen as the product of culture and those which are self-initiated. Was Hitler responsible for his deeds, was he a moral agent or were his actions inevitably shaped by the times and circumstances of his upbringing? Indeed where does human culpability begin—if at all? Was Hitler culpable for his crimes against humanity? What were his motives? From what sinister desires did he will and craft the Final Solution?

Ron Rosenbaum in his book *Explaining Hitler*, repeatedly addresses the question of Hitler as "cultural product or as a "(im)moral agent."[9] He writes of the current tendency to regard anything that hints of a 'Great Man' theory of history as unsophisticated compared with resort to explanation by 'Great Abstractions' such as 'Western racism'.[10] And yet we are confronted with the attempt to understand evil and evildoers. Rosenbaum also provides us with the position of Milton Himmelfarb "who took arms against Great Abstraction theories in a powerful 1984 essay entitled 'No Hitler, No Holocaust'. Himmelfarb's particular target in that essay was the theory that singles out Christian anti-Semitism as the true source of the Holocaust. [He] argues that abstract ideological or theological animus is not sufficient [to explain Hitler's role in the Holocaust]."[11]

For Himmelfarb as for many others Hitler was an evil person whose intentions to exterminate the Jews was a persistent and enduring theme in his mind and consciousness. Rosenbaum refers to the work of Lucy S. Dawidowicz and her 1975 study *The War Against the Jews*.

In forceful but carefully footnoted prose, she makes the case that those who believe Hitler had not made up his mind as late as 1941 are ignorant of the true nature of Hitler's intentions, have been taken in by a cunning con game Hitler played on all but his innermost circle when it came to the question of the Final Solution. Her challenge to the tendency of contemporary scholarship to give us a Hitler who dithered over his decision is not one of degree, not an argument about differences of months, even years; it's an argument over decades. But more than that it's an argument about Hitler's mind.[12]

Rosenbaum writes in the last chapter of his book:

It might be argued that a half century's attempt to "explain" Hitler have served in some sense to avoid confronting the specter of that Hitler, the laughing Hitler, a Hitler fully conscious of his malignancy. A half century of efforts have added to, broadened, deepened, contextualized, historicized our vision of Hitler in many valuable—though also contradictory—ways. But in so doing, they may also have distanced and distracted us from his person, from his personal responsibility, his desire, the fact that, as Milton Himmelfarb put it, he didn't have to kill the Jews, he wasn't merely compelled by abstract forces—rather, he chose to, he *wanted* to. [13]

BIG WORLD - LITTLE WORLD

Is it fair for anyone to think of Thomas Jefferson or Abraham Lincoln as products of their environments—as individuals inevitably shaped by the social and cultural forces at work in their lifetimes? Are Jefferson and Lincoln and their great works formed by historical events, or are they the makers of the history of our nation and the world? If we see both men as products of civilization, then we deny them much of their greatness. As Skinner would suggest, as we take away their personal freedoms to be the people they have become, we also take away their dignity as two of the world's outstanding leaders. Jefferson and Lincoln were great human beings, not because they happened along at the right time, but because their personal convictions and motives changed the times in which they lived and helped form the society in which we live today. By this logic, if there were no Jefferson or Lincoln, the society we know and accept today would be very different. This also can be said of people with sinister motives. And so we may want to consider what the world would be like if minds like Hitler's or Stalin's never existed. A different world. Yes, in all likelihood a very different world. And if this is true in the "big world" out there, it is also true in the "little worlds" we all live in. In a very blunt sense, our own values and convictions make or break our worlds and the worlds of many close to us.

Is this a consoling or fearful thought? Do we want the responsibility of our convictions? Is it too scary to think that we create our own worlds? The existentialist thinker Martin Heidegger contends free decision making is always accompanied by anxiety since there is a quality of the unknown in all the authentic decisions we make. There are also powers and responsibility inherent in such decisions. [14] To live by one's convictions is by this argument living courageously, albeit fearfully. We worry about whether we will be able to act courageously when the situation demands, and we worry about whether we will be able to fulfill so many of life's responsibilities as we and others expect we should. The anxiety that Heidegger elaborates in his philosophy is indeed present in our lives.

Are our personal convictions and motives as important as we think? Is Heidegger's version of anxiety really true, or can we bluff our way along without responsibility and without remorse? If anxiety and remorse are negative emotions, maybe psychology's "happiness brokers" can show us a better way. Maybe they can provide the "out" we need. Maybe we should take the "out" that great thinkers provide, the "out" of behaviorism, the "out" of psychoanalysis, or the "out" of those evolutionary psychologists who accept the idea that human behavior like human biology follows the principles of natural selection.

We can think of civilization as the product of human motivation or as the consequence of overwhelming social-cultural forces (What Rosenbaum refers to as "Great Abstraction Theories"). It is true that some of our greatest ideas ultimately discount the importance of human motivation. Humanity by this "enlightened" view is more product than cause. Great thinkers, philosophers, and scientists with different interests tend to support this view. One of the world's greatest philosophers, Frederick Hegel, viewed civilization as constantly evolving toward higher states of perfection through the dialectical process. His dialectic involved a thesis counteracted by an antithesis which, together formed a new synthesis. This synthesis then became the thesis for a subsequent cycle, repeating the process through time until civilized society approached the highest degree of perfection.

Herbert Spencer also saw civilization as evolving through various stages of development until the highest form of civilization could be achieved. Spencer, who coined the phrase *survival of the fittest*, based his ideas on the evolutionary theory of Charles Darwin. In his view, society would continue to progress as those people most fit to endure would do so and those not so equipped to endure would be eliminated in the natural course of events. This evolutionary process came to be known as *Social Darwinism*, a favorite view of American capitalists such as Andrew Carnegie and John D. Rockefeller. Those not fit to survive were dispensable.[15]

Auguste Comte also saw society as an evolutionary process coining the term *sociology* as his method for comparing different societies as they move through various stages of progress.[16]

Karl Marx, one of the world's most influential political theorists, saw his materialist conception of history as a transformation of Hegel's dialectical process. Marx viewed communism as emerging from a struggle between the bourgeois and the proletariat forces of society.

Deciphering what he conceived to be the hidden meaning-content of Hegel's *Phenomenology of Mind*, Marx here formulated his own conception of history as a process of self-development of the human species culminating in communism. Man, according to his conception, is essentially a producer. . . . In the course of history, which Marx described as a "history of production," a world of created objects gradually arises around man. Original nature is overlaid with man-made or "anthropological nature." And Marx believed that this was the true or scientific restatement of the Hegelian conception.[17]

Freud in his book *Civilization and Its Discontents* explained civilization as the product of repressed unconscious conflicts that seek resolution in a variety of institutional forms and practices.[18] The author has provided his own views on this issue:

The problem is that civilization provides no antidote for the original urgings of the libido—merely substitute satisfactions that call upon the same energy source. Civilization, therefore, restricts sexual activity to its own designs. Freud does not say so, but where these are scarce resources there is inevitable conflict.

But there's a more powerful conflict which helps explain the destructive force of civilization. It is seen in the fact that sex is not the one primary instinct. There is another which causes civilization endless woe. There is the instinct of aggressiveness. To protect itself from the destructive force of human aggressiveness, civilization necessarily employs a high level of energy to hold aggressiveness in check. While it has succeeded in some measure, history clearly shows that civilization has repeatedly witnessed humanity's inhumanity. "Civilization has to use its utmost efforts in order to set limits to man's aggressive instincts and to hold the manifestations of them in check by psychical reaction-formations. Hence, therefore, the use of methods intended to incite people into identifications and aim-inhibited relationships of love, hence the restriction upon sexual life, and hence too the ideal's commandment to love one's neighbour as one's self—a commandment which is really justified by the fact that nothing runs so strongly counter to the original nature of man." Love of one's neighbor according to Freud is totally incompatible with human nature—elsewhere he says that it is much more natural to hate our neighbor and so human nature reveals itself in this perennial duel between humanity and civilization. . . . Civilized humanity is in effect betrayed by its own nature in its quest for happiness.[19]

Or so Freud would have us believe.

For all these thinkers, whether Hegel, Marx, or Freud, human will and intentionality are submerged by overwhelming sociocultural forces, and the person comes into the world irretrievably shaped by these forces. For the postmodernists the fact that these forces are objective and outside the person represent the mistaken idea that truth is "out there" somewhere and requires the construction of various paradigms to achieve human understanding. Fred Newman and Lois Holzman in their book *The End of Knowing*, state the following:

The nearly complete domination of philosophy by epistemology that occurred during this century [which includes Hegel, Freud and others]. . . has had the effect of muting the critically important distinction between having a conceptual framework (a way of knowing, a path, a view, a theory) for engaging the world or reality and *actively engaging* [italics mine] the world or reality. The result is the typically unstated assumption that human engagement is made possible by world views theoretical constructs, and abstractions.[20]

They then state their postmodern position as follows:

As we see it, the target of the postmodern critique only appears to be epistemology—that is, knowing as the dominant mode of understanding. . . . We argue in this book that in order for postmodernism to become world historic (revolutionary) it must make a direct attack "against epistemology". . . . A revolutionary shift beyond modernism entails moving beyond epistemology (frames of mind, points of view) altogether.[21]

Heidegger's epistemology, concedes the inevitability of environmental forces in his concept of "throwness," but he never abandons the human capacity to form personal life decisions—to exercise one's personal freedom in constructing a meaningful life.[22] Heidegger's philosophy allows us to appreciate the influence of this world around us while also underscoring the truth of human freedom. For Freud, history is the maker of the human condition. For Heidegger, humanity is the maker of history.

The course of civilization can be understood best as an account of human motivation, and each person instinctually looks to the past to understand one's personhood. We are all preoccupied with history, the history of one's people, the history of one's land, one's personal history. But why are we so curious about the past? Is not the perennial question for each human, human nature itself? And is not human nature best revealed in history? Were Yale University experiments on obedience necessary to tell us to what lengths humans will go out of sense of obedience to authority? Hasn't history told us that time and time again?

With all due respect to the work of Dr. Milgram, in many cases the knowledge gained is identical, whether from experimentation or from history. Experimenters know that truth is best established by replicating the results—by conducting the experiment again at a different time and place, with different participants, and by a different experimenter. Does history not itself provide a more dramatic replication of human behavior than can ever be achieved in a laboratory? History is a compelling tale of humanity's free acts. The highest moments in history are stories of human heroism and courage—when the individual overcame great odds so that one's motives could be enacted—a Mahatma Gandhi, a Martin Luther King, a Jackie Robinson.

Humankind is the creator of history. There is not one history but many stories, many accounts from age to age and continent to continent. But always there is human striving, human passion, and suffering, the conqueror and the vanquished, the oppressor and the oppressed, the loved and the unloved.

One useful definition of time (and there are many definitions—at least one for every philosopher who ever lived) is that time is the measurement of change. By this definition, change is seen as the ultimate determinant of time, and in a sense, change and time are the necessary coordinates of all experience. History is the record of human experience, and it is useful, then, to think of history not as "times past" but as antecedent change, change still unraveling itself into the future. It is most important also to understand that humans are responsible for their history as well as their future—that humanity created the past just as humanity inevitably will shape the future. The human is the central figure in history. Humans establish laws and institutions. They produce works of art. They record their experiences in written history and literature. They penetrate the physical laws of the universe and jump to the planets. Humankind is always on the move, insatiably curious, ever exploring the world and reaching beyond. In the very best sense, humanity creates change, and human beings are the prime movers of the times in which they live. Charles Mitchell discusses William James's views on this very point:

Pragmatism brings together the key elements of James's philosophy: The world is pluralistic; it is composed of "an indefinitely numerous lot of *eaches*" who participate in the construction of reality. . . (602). The result is a world defined by its impermanence, one that always resists our efforts to pin it down as fixed and absolute. In turn, the pragmatic theory of truth maintains that it is precisely within this mutable reality that individual effort most clearly manifests itself: "In our cognitive as well as in our active life we are creative. We *add*, both to the subject and to the predicate part of reality. The world stands really malleable waiting to receive its final touches at our hands. . . . Man engenders truth upon it."(599) For James, pluralism, radical empiricism, and pragmaticism work together to emphasize the supreme importance of each individual to the world in which we live, a world that is essentially of our own making.[23]

It is most important, therefore, to understand the nature of change and how humankind is the substantive cause of historical change. This frees us from the trap set by the environmentalists and the determinists—whose cart, well equipped as it may be, is indeed before the horse. Certainly the makers of history require more psychological understanding than Skinner's pigeons can ever, ever provide.

How has humanity used its precious time, its "mortal coil"?

This is the question for history, but it is really close to the question of human motivation as well. It is also tragically true that empirical psychology has for the most part overlooked history. Although motivational theorists make a great deal out of each individual's intrapsychic past, very little has been done to understand human nature by studying the historical past. Henry Ford is quoted as saying that "history is bunk." Unfortunately, many psychologists seem to have much the same opinion of history. Sadly, psychology's resistance to the study of history probably rests in its preoccupation with itself as a science.

Skinner admits that as a psychologist, he is not really interested in historical evidence. For the behaviorist, the experimental laboratory is far better suited to gaining an understanding of human nature than the subjective accounts of historians who project their own biases into the pages they write. Since psychology is a science, historical analysis simply has no place in psychological investigation. Moreover, historical accounts are inherently unreliable. In his last book, Carl Sagan argues eloquently for the cause of science and scientific verification, but he also feels that an understanding of history has much to offer in our search for truth. He writes:

The methods of science—with all its imperfections—can be used to improve social, political, and economic systems, and this is, I think, true no matter what criterion of improvement is adapted. How is this possible if science is based on experiment? Humans are not electrons or laboratory rats. But every act of Congress, every Supreme Court decision, every Presidential National Security Directive, every change in the Prime Rate is an experiment. Every shift in economic policy, every increase or decrease in funding for Head Start, every toughening of criminal sentences is an experiment. Exchanging needles, making condoms freely available, or decriminalizing marijuana are all experiments. Doing nothing to help Abyssinia against Italy, or to prevent Nazi Germany from invading the Rhineland was an experiment. . . .Handguns are available for self-protection in Seattle but not in nearby Vancouver, Canada; handgun killings are five times more common and the handgun suicide rate is ten times greater in Seattle. Guns make impulsive killing easy. This is also an experiment. In almost all these cases adequately controlled experiments are not performed, or variables are insufficiently separated. Nevertheless, to a certain and often useful degree, policy ideas can be tested. The great waste would be to ignore the results of social experiments because they seem to be ideologically unpalatable.[24]

Although history is, ipso facto, outside the reach of science, the trade-offs in favor of behavioral science hardly seem worth the tragic loss to psychology of five thousand years of recorded history. Do we simply ignore the evidence of history because historical facts are not "scientific" facts? Is the role of psychological science to establish the laws of human behavior, or to contribute to the betterment of the human condition—or both? Taking a fuller account of historical evidence should be important to the achievement of both objectives; indeed, the second objective cannot be met without historical testimony.

HUMAN NATURE AND THE NATURE OF CHANGE

Let's look further at humanity and change by investigating first the nature of change. There are four dimensions of change. First, change is critical or it is incidental, it is significant in its consequences or relatively unimportant in the larger scheme of things. Secondly, change is relatively permanent and enduring or its effects are transitory. Thirdly, change is widespread or local in its effects, it can encompass nation, continent, or the world, or it can be held to a small area. Finally, and most important from the point of view of motivation, change can be purposeful or accidental. Some change is intentional and in line with human planning, whereas other change happens accidentally or despite human planning. Clearly, then, the greatest figures in history are those who have purposefully created change—change that has been substantial, widespread, and enduring in its effects. The study of history when viewed this way is the study of change wrought by humanity. As Emerson says and as most biographers would likely agree, the most fascinating aspect of biography is human motivation, especially of those gigantic figures who by their motives have changed the world.

At this point, it might be interesting to put the book aside for a moment and on a separate piece of paper, jot down your selection of the ten most important figures in Western civilization—those people who, by their lives and their motives, have purposefully generated change of great consequence. Take some time and think about it. Remember that there are many figures in history who have accomplished great feats—a Charles Lindbergh, for example—but who do not rank among the great historical figures because their accomplishments, although considerable, were less than gigantic in moving the world in the direction it has taken. One test you might use in coming up with your list is to speculate on the world had certain people never lived. Jesus Christ, for example. Suppose Jesus had never lived. Would the world be any different? No doubt the world would be vastly different today had Jesus Christ never lived. Now take a moment and compile your list of the ten most important figures in all of history—who because of their power, ideas, art, or virtue, have changed the world. Because of his singular importance in Western culture, Jesus Christ has been omitted from the list that appears below. Make your selections before reading this list.

If you compare your list with this one, you probably will find some names that appear on both—but there are some people who will not appear on both lists. What matters is not the names, but the realization that individuals have made history by the power of their personal motivations, in the exercise of their freedom as human beings and in the exercise of their will. The point is made elsewhere in this book that the shape of the future and our destiny as a human race will be a function of what humanity *decides to do* with its talents and with its knowledge. Talent and knowledge must be willfully put to use by people. Indeed, it is this actualization of talent and knowledge that will change the world.

It makes little difference if we live in a slow- or fast-paced world. What matters is human dignity, mutual respect, compassion, cooperation, and opportunities for human growth and self-realization. Human progress can no longer be defined in terms of technological or even scientific advances. Human progress cannot be seen in how "smart" we have become. Rather, it must be seen in terms of human potential for growth, creativity, expression, interaction, and happiness.

Newman and Holzman state the following:

We are. . . not denying that human beings structure the world, create theoretical constructs, conceptual frameworks, or engage in abstraction (such as interpretation and explanation). Nor do we think that these capacities are in themselves problematic. We are suggesting, however, that we human beings do these things far less than philosophers, scientists and social scientists have led us to believe. Moreover, this all-persuasive cognitive bias has brought our species dangerously close to developmental paralysis.[25]

Human destiny rests not in human intelligence but in human will and direction; it is not knowledge and skill but motives which will make the future.

Aristotle	(384–322 B.C.)
Luther	(1483–1546)
Newton	(1642–1727)
Washington	(1732–1799)
Jefferson	(1743–1826)
Darwin	(1809–1882)
Einstein	(1863–1955)
Lenin	(1870–1924)
Hitler	(1889–1945)
Gorbachev	(1931–)

A defense of this list is not made here. We probably all agree that these are important historical figures who have made an enormous impact on the course of history. Your list undoubtedly consists of ten similar personalities whose contribution to history is undeniable.

The purpose of this exercise is not to come up with a consensus on a list of names. Rather, the purpose is to illustrate how history itself has been influenced by just a few people in such significant ways. In the preface to his book, *The Biology of Moral Systems*, Richard Alexander proposes the view that the will of one person can change the world. "No matter how many millions of citizens may exist in a given nation-state, no matter how hideous its weaponry, the decision regarding the use of that weaponry eventually comes down to about the same small number of individuals, or even to the calculations of single brain. At least as a final step, it takes only one finger to push a button that could bring on what might aptly be termed the ultimate holocaust."[26]

It makes a great deal of difference whether humans are motivated by power or by virtue—whether the person is concerned with indulging one's ego or expending it. A psychology that simply explains behavior like an engineer explains the workings of a machine is not satisfactory. We must have a psychology that is equally concerned with human values and is unafraid to evaluate the content of human motivation. Maslow writes brilliantly on this point.

The human being needs a framework of values, a philosophy of life, a religion or religion-surrogate to live by and understand by, in about the same sense that he needs sunlight, calcium or love. This I call the 'cognitive need to understand.' The value-illnesses which result from valuelessness are called variously anhedonia, anomie, apathy, amorality, hopelessness, cynicism, etc. and can become somatic illness as well. Historically we are in a value interregnum in which all externally given value systems have proven to be failures (political, economic, religious, etc.) e.g., nothing is worth dying for. What man needs but he doesn't have, he seeks for unceasingly, and he becomes dangerously ready to jump at any hope, good or bad. The cure for this disease is obvious. We need a validated, usable system of human values that we can believe in and devote ourselves to (be willing to die for), because they are true rather than because we are exhorted to 'believe and have faith.' Such an empirically based Weltanschauung seems now to be a real possibility, at least in theoretical outline.[27]

What good is psychological science unless it concerns itself ultimately with the betterment of the human condition? This is not an individual matter; it is a matter that concerns all of us equally. This is more a question of human motivation than anything else. It is, therefore, ultimately a question for psychology. Mitchell, on this point, reminds us of William James's contention: "Indeed, James advances his idea of pluralism primarily as a means of calling our attention to the worth of other individuals rather than simply promoting our need to liberate ourselves. Pluralism stresses a plurality of independent selves working interdependently. . . . For James, the 'workshop of being' is always a cooperative affair. . . ."[28]

HISTORY AND THEMATIC MOTIVATION

If humans are motivated to power and pleasure, they will certainly destroy the environment and there will be no escape. If they are motivated to self-actuation, they will investigate the environment and possibly enhance its riches. If they are motivated by love, they will enjoy the environment with others who will also take joy in it. The technical and scientific advances that have led to the harnessing of atomic energy is certainly an example of man's genius and his creative intellectual capacity. Wonderful! But the question remains: How will man use this great discovery? There already have been two atomic holocausts, not to mention the atmospheric pollution from hundreds of "experimental bombs" and nuclear leaks. We have learned recently of the polluting effects of nuclear testing and how nuclear fallout has been mapped throughout the United States. We have seen how human motivation can work against humanity, but we also observe how it can work for humanity. Our future as a human race depends upon human motivation. It is a problem of eternal consequences. It is a problem that must be solved in our favor; and it can be solved in our favor only out of the good will of each human being to his fellow being. It is mandatory, therefore, that we understand human motivation so that, it is hoped, we can begin to utilize our capacities in ways beneficent to human survival and in keeping with our dignity and our destiny, William James's "workshop of being."

Let's reassess, then, statements made earlier about motivation and human fulfillment. We have established that thematic motivation has three ways to go. The ego can go about indulging itself, expanding itself, or expending itself. Self indulgence is seen in the forms of power or pleasure. Ego-gratifying motivations are exploitative or punishing of others, and lives dominated by this motive are both self-corrupting and corrupting of others. Think how the human race suffers at the hands of people so possessed. Think of the misery and the exploitation. Such motivation can lead only to disaster for *all* involved, and the human race moves another gradual step toward its own annihilation.

A second form of thematic motivation, self-actuation, can be helpful to others. True, many times it is, but it doesn't have to be. Such motivation can simply exist without concern for others and be selfish and self-directed without being exploitative. The self-actuated individual can become so preoccupied with his or her own need system that he or she can forget others or, worse, ignore or reject others. We know that this frequently happens, often accompanied by a certain pomposity, indignation, or conceit and sometimes a disdain for the unlearned and less capable.

Of course it is true that the self-actuated individual frequently is involved in creative production that works ultimately to the betterment of humankind; the arts and sciences are typically the result of the self-actuated individual, and humanity has profited immeasurably from such efforts. It is impossible to estimate the enormous strides made out of actuation of human creative potential. The point, however, is that human destiny cannot count on it, because human advancement is not a *first principle* of self-actuation motivation. It is often, fortunately, a corollary principle but not a first principle. Self-actuation motivation must be moderated by altruistic motivation for humanity to profit in the long run. Mitchell refers us to the final chapter of James's *Pragmatism*, "[I]in our world, the wishes of the individual are only one condition. Other individuals are there with other wishes and they must be propitiated first."[29]

It is interesting that great motivational theorists such as Abraham Maslow and David McClelland, from whom we have learned so much about human nature and human values, devote so much attention to individual needs for achievement, recognition, esteem, and self-fulfillment, and insufficient attention to the question of mutuality and human welfare. Yet Maslow's theory of motivation has endured more than fifty years and is still very popular. The person, according to Maslow, to use his own term, is a *wanting animal*. This hardly conjures up a sense of giving or sharing. One does not expend oneself in the service of others by being a "wanting animal." Maslow would likely argue that the individual can choose to actualize the self through helping and aiding others—that living for others is one way of actualizing the self. In his later writings, he includes helping others among the gratifications of self-actualizing people.[30] But the self remains central to his thinking, and it is the self that seeks actualization, the self that must endure and be enhanced. In suggesting that people live to enhance the self and that the self is constantly wanting, Maslow provides a tenuous rationale for people who live not for self but in spite of self. If Maslow also saw the person as a "giving animal," how much different his theory would be!

McClelland's very important theory of achievement motivation also is constructed around the self—a self that is self-centered and self-indulging.[31] McClelland describes the individual high in *achievement motivation* as someone who (1) wants personal responsibility for solving problems (and the opportunity for credit and recognition that goes with it); (2) takes moderate risks to optimize ego satisfaction with minimal risk of failure; and (3) needs feedback on how well one is doing. Doesn't this sound like an extremely self-centered individual to you? One probably would not want to be an obstacle in such a person's way as he or she pushed forward from achievement to achievement—although if they felt that being a "good friend" would aid their cause of success, they would probably find time to be nice. Of course, achievement motivation is nothing new despite McClelland's "discoveries." "Yond Cassius" did have "a lean and hungry look" and such men are indeed "dangerous." Incidentally, the difference between Brutus and Cassius rests not in their deeds but in their motives. For Cassius, it was clearly a matter of power, whereas Brutus was concerned for the people of Rome. They were totally different men—different by their motives. Marc Antony knew the difference:

All the conspirators save only he,

Did that they did in envy of great Caesar;

He only, in a general honest thought

And common good to all, made one of them.

His life was gentle, and the elements

So mixed in him that Nature might stand up

And say to all the world "This was a man!"[32]

(Marc Antony may have made the best statement for self-actualization in all of literature, including Maslow.)

Obviously, all motivation theories have to begin with the self, but not all theories need view the self as ceaselessly wanting, interminably in need, and always seeking self-indulgence. Such theories see humanity in very selfish terms—the selfish genes at work. Freud does and so does Maslow. History provides innumerable examples of people not as taking but as giving, not as seeking but as surrendering, not as dominating but as yielding. A mature human being can give up one's life for a friend; courage and selflessness must be possible alternatives for humanity. Do we need another controlled experiment to measure this phenomenon? Can Skinner's pigeons ever, ever tell us anything of human courage? Can Milgram's research ever tell of heroism? Do such experiments really tell us anything at all that history has not told us and continues to tell us better?

NOTES

1. Stanley Milgram, "Some Conditions of Obedience and Disobedience to Authority," *Human Relations* 18 (1965), 57–76.

2. Ibid., 60.

3. Ibid., 62 (footnote 6).

4. Ibid., 72.

5. Ibid., 66.

6. Arthur G. Miller, *The Obedience Experiments* (New York: Praeger, 1986), 124.

7. Rom Harré, *Social Being: A Theory for Social Psychology* (Oxford: Basil Blackwell, 1979), 106.

8. Lewis W. Brandt, "Don't Sweep the Ethical Problems under the Rug! Totalitarian Versus Equalitarian Ethics," *Canadian Psychological Review* 19 (1978), 65.

9. Ron Rosenbaum, *Explaining Hitler: The Search for the Origins of His Evil* (New York: Random House, 1998), xiii.

10. Ibid., xiii.

11. Ibid., xiii.

12. Ibid., 373.

13. Ibid., 389.

14. Hergenhahn, 513 (see chap. 3, n. 11).

15. Ibid., 265.

16. Ibid., 148.

17. Robert C. Tucker, ed., *The Marx-Engels Reader* (New York: W. W. Norton & Co., 1978), xxiv.

18. Sigmund Freud, *Civilization and Its Discontents*. (see chap. 2, n. 4).

19. "Freud's Civilization and Its Discontents," Robert P. Cavalier, Dana Lecture Series, Elmira College, March 1988. See Freud, *Civilization and Its Discontents*, 66.

20. Fred Newman and Lois Holzman, *The End of Knowing* (New York: Routledge, 1997), 8.

21. Ibid., 10–11.

22. Hergenhahn, 513 (see chap. 3, n. 11).

23. Charles E. Mitchell, *Individualism and Its Discontents: Appropriations of Emerson, 1880–1950* (Amherst, Mass.: University of Massachusetts Press, 1997), 94–95. Quotations taken from William James, *Pragmatism* (referenced pages).

24. Carl Sagan, *The Demon-Haunted World* (New York: Ballantine Books, 1996), 423.

25. Fred Newman and Lois Holzman, *The End of Knowing*, 9.

26. Alexander, xiii (see chap. 4, n. 5).

27. Abraham H. Maslow, *Toward a Psychology of Being* (Princeton: Van Nostrand, 1962), 192.

28. Mitchell, 102–103.

29. Ibid., 101, quotation from William James, *Pragmatism*.

30. Maslow, *Farther Reaches of Human Nature*, 297(see chap. 5, n. 22).

31. David McClelland, *Human Motivation* (Glenview, Ill.: Scott, Foresman and Co., 1985), 223–267. McClelland also reports that people high in achievement motivation were more innovative, especially if this resulted in more efficiency or more opportunity to perform well. Unfortunately, he also reports that such people are more likely to cheat.

32. *Julius Caesar* 4.574–81.

CHAPTER 7

Territories Within

And yet no weapons—no matter how powerful—can help the West until it overcomes its loss of willpower.

—Aleksandr Solzhenitsyn
(Address upon receiving honorary Doctor of Letters at Harvard University commencement, 15 June, 1978)

On two separate occasions this author bought a plastic garbage can to replace a broken one in the kitchen. In both cases, the new cans were too big, a result of a faulty estimation of the size of the previous cans. This happened in spite of awareness of the *garbage can illusion*, an illusion hit upon a few years before while teaching a class in human perception. It has been demonstrated many times in both undergraduate and graduate courses and once with Rick Wesp at a professional conference on the Teaching of Psychology.[1] It is very easy to demonstrate. Simply place a typical classroom garbage can (The one used was fourteen inches high) on a table before a group of people and ask that they record their estimates of the height and width of the can. Even though it is a relatively simple perceptual task, people tend to overestimate the height of a fourteen-inch can but not the width. Height estimates of twenty inches or more are not uncommon.

The illusion is so consistent across groups that the findings have been published.[2] We have also used students as co-investigators in follow-up studies that demonstrate that such errors are relatively commonplace for other familiar objects.[3] Such illusions restrict us from seeing the world as it actually is. Perceptual distortions happen even though reason tells us otherwise. For example, in Figure 2, which line is longer, the top or bottom line?[4] Seeing is not always believing. Misperceptions, mistakes, errors in judgment, and forgetfulness are part of human nature. Truth and certainty are elusive, and our searches have taken us down many blind alleys. Our freedom to access truth and gain knowledge is theoretically present, but such understanding is not so easily achieved. As we are free to gain truth, we are also free to make mistakes. In Figure 2 the top and bottom lines are equal in length.

Figure 2

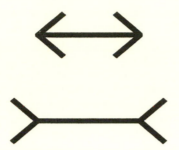

The Müller-Lyer Illusion

Indeed, the fact that humans make so many mistakes and follow so many false leads is testimony to our freedom. A cat is far less prone to mistakes than a person is. As a cat's access to truth is limited, so is his tendency toward error. He has less freedom and has no moral judgment whatsoever. Although he may make the "right" decision to stay inside when it is very cold out and it is "good" for him that he do so, there is no right or wrong or good or bad for the cat—not in the moral sense. But there sure is for people. The whole moral order that's found in the world is based on human capacity to choose and decide.

Moral decisions are the highest expression of freedom in the world, but all parts of nature have a certain kind of natural freedom, even when there is little or no capacity to choose or decide. In this sense, a chair has freedom, a bird has freedom, the planet Uranus has freedom, and each living person has freedom. Death and destruction destroy freedom, but time does, too. As time decays, it destroys freedom.

When rocks impregnable, are not so stout,
Nor gates of steel so strong, but Time decays.[5]

Freedom is precious as life is precious. But is a chair free, the book in your hands? Do these inanimate, dumb objects possess freedom? No, certainly not in the sense that humanity possesses freedom, yet we know also that humanity is not entirely free. Humans are limited by the laws of nature and by their own human nature. The human being uses time to reason, to build, to live (that same time that decays) and, as one uses time, one is in a sense burning out one's freedom. People are not infused with the knowledge of the universe. They must study, they must learn, they must work. They are not completely free. They misperceive, misjudge, and make mistakes. There are constraints. Human intelligence is as much a constraint to freedom as it is a source of freedom, for intelligence is both limited and limiting. The cognitive psychologist Jerry Fodor has a term for this kind of mental limitation. He calls it *epistemic boundedness*.[6]

But certainly humans have freedom to decide—to choose to activate their own essence, as the existentialists might say. The human being is a willing creature. Chairs and books do not choose; they do not decide. They do not have free will. For humanity, creative activity actualizes freedom; they are one and the same. Humans are most free when they create. Indeed, as the creator is free, the created is free—because as an expression of will it has freedom. An example of this principle may be seen in works of art. A sunset, although beautiful, is not a work of art until it is captured by the artist's brush. And what is captured by the artist is not merely color and form; rather, it is the transcendental attribute of nature, nature's freedom that can be captured only by another free being. The artist, the sculptor, the writer is free to do whatever he or she decides in the creative act. There are no constraints but the physical dimensions of the medium itself (the canvas, the marble, the paper), and the product is art if it expresses the freedom within the artist. Imagine a painter who was told at gunpoint exactly what to draw, line by line, color by color. The product, no matter how beautiful, would not be art. Painting by numbers is another good example of non-art, in which the painter is given a canvas preprinted with numbers to represent different colors—the result is definitely not art. Freedom is essential to art. The difference between a good and bad painting is the freedom impressed into the work by the creative artist. A great artist captures the freedom of nature in a variety of forms whether it be painting, dance, architecture, or drama. That which is mechanical is not free, and therefore, a computer cannot create a work of art because it is lacking, not so much in talent, but in the freedom to creatively deploy that talent. A computer may think, but it does not have a self that wills.

In his book *The Meaning of the Creative Act*, Nicolas Berdyaev states it this way:

Creativity is inseparable from freedom. Only he who is free creates. Out of necessity can be born only evolution, creativity is born of liberty. When we speak in our imperfect human language about creativity out of nothing, we are really speaking of creativity out of freedom. . . . Creativity is inexplicable: creativity is the mystery of freedom. The mystery of freedom is immeasurably deep and inexplicable. Just as deep and inexplicable is the mystery of creativity. . . . Creativity is something which proceeds from within, out of immeasurable and inexplicable depths, not from without, not from the world's necessity.[7]

Freedom, its activity and its source, is a gut issue in psychology and philosophy and now also in biology. If, indeed, humankind is free, it makes a great deal of difference in both the theoretical and practical order of things. The social and ethical implications are obvious. To deny human freedom is to surrender to pure expediency and "might will be right" after all. The idea of democracy is, after all, dependent on the idea of human freedom.

The humanistic psychology expressed in this text maintains that humans are different from other animals—that human nature is *essentially* different from the nature of the beasts. And because humans are different from the other animals, human nature must be studied in and of itself. A basic premise of humanistic psychology is that human nature cannot be adequately understood by the study of other animals, be it rat, pigeon, or ape. Human beings can decide what's important in life and how they want to live. Humans can choose love over hate, knowledge over ignorance, beauty over ugliness, hope over despair. As a willing being, the human person cannot be sufficiently understood by studying animal behavior. Animal freedom, to the extent that it exists, is temporal and physical. Animals do not make decisions that invest life with meaning. Animals do not transcend time and place. They have no literature; they have no art.

As Skinner says, a difference is not a difference unless it makes a difference. Certainly it makes a great deal of difference if we view humanity and human nature as unique, if we try to understand humans as humans and not simply as reacting organisms. This is more than a matter of evolved human intelligence as Carl Sagan would have it and is much more a matter of human willing—a point missed by Sagan.[8]

For humanity, freedom rests in the capacity to decide—not merely to choose which coat to wear, which school to attend, or which person to marry, but rather, one's personal meaning in living. Humanity is capable of infusing life with meaning and value. Moreover, man and woman are capable of procreating, of having children and knowing the joy of parenthood. Humans can also reject, ignore, destroy, and kill. They soon may be able to clone themselves. For each person, freedom is an awesome concept tied not simply to one's dignity but to one's personal destiny and the life and destiny of others. It is for this reason that we have laws. Without freedom, there is no morality, no ethics, and no reason for our laws.

A chimpanzee does not have free will. It possesses freedom in a unidimensional way appropriate to its nature. It can choose in the physical order of things to eat, to drink, to sleep, to run, or not to do any of these things. It can be defiant and stubborn, but it cannot decide "to be or not to be." The human being can choose the terms of existence. Humans can will "to be or not to be." Human decision making is discussed more fully in Chapter 8.

CONSCIOUSNESS

Willing is always a conscious act. Willing is the opposite of habit, although acts that were initially voluntary can become habitual, sometimes with dire consequences. When we lose conscious control of our own behavior we can put ourselves at high risk. Consciousness and self-control are reciprocal features of human willing and come close to defining our humanity. Bernard Baars writes:

When behaviorists in science and philosophy expelled consciousness about 1900, they also turned away from the two sister issues of voluntary control and self. . . . Volition has been neglected as long as consciousness, in part because it has been difficult to show that voluntary control involves a difference that makes a difference. . . . [However,] everyone knows the difference between a spontaneous smile and a voluntary one. Spontaneous smiles seem to happen to us; voluntary ones are planned. Paul Ekman is the best known pioneer in detailed studies of facial expressions and has exhaustively catalogued the muscle movements that make up emotional expressions. Ekman and coworkers consistently find that spontaneous expressions, such as genuine smiles, are visibly different from voluntary ones. . . . Voluntary actions are not just complicated agglomerations of simple reflexes; involuntary components put together do not result in a voluntary act. Something else is involved in voluntary control.[9]

Baars also argues that consciousness must be present in voluntary acts. Acts that are no longer conscious—which lose self-control—can sometimes be perilous:

One reason to make goals and places conscious is that automaticity is a great source of error. The British cognitive psychologist James Reason (1984) has analyzed catastrophic accidents in which fatalities were apparently caused by misplaced automaticity: a London bus driver who crashed a double-decker bus into a low overpass, killing six passengers—perhaps because he was in the habit of driving the same route in a single-decker bus: a train collision killing ninety people because the driver made a habitual turn, but this time onto the wrong track.[10]

Human freedom is seated in consciousness. It is within this self-awareness that the individual experiences the capacity to move and shape one's existence. Franz Brentano's views on intentionality are interesting in this regard. Rollo May in his book *Love and Will* discusses his ideas: "Brentano believed that consciousness is defined by the fact that it intends something outside itself—specifically that it intends the object. Thus intentionality gives meaningful content to consciousness."[11] This is very close to what has been said here—that freedom and creativity are somehow united in consciousness. In fact, freedom and creativity may be co-principles of human consciousness, for as William James wrote one hundred years ago, "The pursuance of future ends and the choice of means for their attainment are thus the mark and criterion of the presence of mentality in a phenomenon."[12] This awareness is inherently personal and private and is beyond the reach of empirical science. Human self-consciousness also seems to be different than animal consciousness. Humans know as animals know. The difference is that humans know that they know. This puts humans into a new dimension of reality apparently not shared by animals and other forms of life. It is in this dimension, through power to know the activity of one's own thought, that the individual must also be possessed with the capacity to decide. It is here that human will is experienced, for if the individual could not will, if one could not decide, the person would be caught in the redundancy of one's self-awareness and would be drawn into infinity like mirrors face to face, unable to escape the inevitable reflection of image on image, self on self. But humans can direct knowing and can deploy consciousness to their own motives. They can plan, they can recant, they can start again.

An interesting example of this, so simply stated yet so very profound, was on the TV show "Sesame Street" many years ago. The character Bob had decided to play a "mirror game" with Big Bird. Bob's instructions were simple: he asked Big Bird to pretend that he was looking into a mirror. Every time Bob would perform a gesture, Big Bird was to imitate it. Such fun! Big Bird was thrilled to participate in such a game. So Bob bowed from the waist, and Big Bird bowed from the waist. Bob raised his arms, and Big Bird raised his "arms." Bob laughed, and Big Bird laughed. The game was a delight. Bob said, "The game is over," and Big Bird said, "The game is over." Bob repeated, "No, really, it's over," and Big Bird replied in kind, "No, really, it's over." "It's over, Big Bird!" exclaimed Bob. "It's over, Big Bird!" shouted Big Bird.

Whatever Bob did or said, Big Bird repeated or imitated. There was no way out for Bob or Big Bird, and according to the rules, the game would last forever. There was only one solution, and it was up to Big Bird. He had to decide not to continue. The conditions were established for infinity, but Big Bird could will his way out of the dilemma. He could not reason his way out, since reason dictated only the futility of playing forever. Big Bird, however, could will his way out of the game if he decided to do so.

And so it is with humanity. Confronted with "the inevitable," humans can still decide. This is both the power and awesomeness of human freedom. It is this awesome power, this consideration of one's being, that is human in the ultimate sense. It is for this reason that to understand humanity, we must begin with humans, not pigeons. The consequence of human motivation is, simply stated, the future of the human race. We have known a holocaust. Will there be another? Humanity must will it not to be. The human race has already created the means to its own destruction. The question is whether humanity *will* or *will not* use them.

TECHNOLOGY AND CREATIVITY

Technology is upon us fast and hard and it's not about to let go. The world is full of labor-saving, work-creating devices—computers are a constant example. Humans today are faster, more reliable, and more accurate than ever. Thanks to the machine, amazing feats are possible; the planets are now within our reach, and radar waves traverse the universe, reaching for intergalaxial rationality. The best-made machines are incredible for their accuracy, reliability, and durability. Machines have made it possible for humanity not only to extend the human capacity to a limitless world without, but to probe that limitless world within. Computers not only direct the course of spacecraft to Mars, Jupiter, and Pluto, they also provide wondrous insight into human reasoning itself. This has resulted in a debate among cognitive psychologists interested in artificial intelligence, so-called AI theorists. The strong AI psychologists see computer thinking and human thinking as two forms of the same process, one done by a computer, the other done by a brain. Thought is thought in both cases, and they are equivalent in value. Weak AI psychologists see human thought as qualitatively different from computer thought because computers can never get to the meaning behind the thought. Alan M. Turing, who founded the field of artificial intelligence, has proposed that if computers can think in ways that cannot be distinguished from human thought, they then pass the *Turing test* and can be said to think. John Searle's famous "Chinese Room" argument refutes the strong AI position.[13] In either case, strong AI or weak AI, computers not only do intelligent things, they represent intelligence itself. As the human does to the computer, the computer does to the human—and so computers that "think" do indeed teach us how we think. A great deal has been discovered on how humans process information and store and retrieve data—perception, cognition, memory, and forgetting are being analyzed and understood, thanks to the computer. Human and machine have fashioned a new partnership that has enormous implications for both doing and knowing. (Hidden in the wings, however, is the question, is it a partnership or is it a race, and if it is a race, who will win?)

But what is a machine? It is utterly contingent upon human design. It has no independent existence. It has no awareness, no self-consciousness, no self-reflection, no will. From whence does it derive its awesome capacity, if not from the humans who made it? Every machine was invented and created by humans or by a machine made by humans. A machine is no more or less than an extension of human powers. Machines are extensions of human physical and intellectual abilities. An individual may be able to press in a thumbtack with one's thumb, but a nail most certainly requires a hammer. A person may be able to turn a screw with a fingernail, but not for long, and never to drive it home. Hammer and screwdriver extend human ability; so do rulers and calculators and computers.

All machines are designed to do work, which humans regard as desirable, and although individuals have invented machines to ease their burden, ultimately the same machines have themselves become a burden. The assembly line is an excellent case in point. In the interest of greater productivity at lower cost, automobile manufacturers use assembly line methods where the human role is to "keep the line moving." To do this, industrial engineers have reduced human capacity to mathematical formulations, so that human error is held to a minimum and decision making is virtually eliminated. When "on-the-line," the industrial worker is not deciding or creating, but simply ordering events in a pre-established way. The decisions and creative work have already been done. The assembly line worker does not wonder what the car would look like if the headlights were lowered or the instrument panel rearranged, or if the worker does wonder, it's not for long, since such wondering is futile. A sad commentary, of course, is that Aristotle and Einstein were right when they said that all knowledge begins in wondering.

Machines have systematically deprived humans of their creative reasoning, of their critical judgment, their decision making, yes, even their sense of reality in many ways. Some computers even tell you whom to date and whether your marriage will work. On a larger scale, computers program traffic patterns on the ground and in the air, and satellites look at the weather from the top rather than from the bottom. Humans have surrendered so much of their reasoning to machines that there is a deficit in human judgment. If the mountaintops look close but the altimeter reading is OK, what does the pilot do, trust his eyes or the altimeter? In fact, people have learned to trust the machine in many ways above their own judgment.

"But, officer, my speedometer read 55 miles per hour."
"That's funny, the gauge read a quarter of a tank."
"Sorry, but according to the timer, this roast should have been done."
"According to my watch, the train should still be here."

In so many seemingly insignificant ways, our freedom has been diminished by the technical age in which we live. The worker on the assembly line knows this, but so does the marketing manager who'd love to play a hunch and open a new territory even though his computer says the opposite.

Human intelligence has created wondrous contraptions that do marvelous things, but they have added a burden to humanity in that they diminish the freedom to choose. They do expand alternatives, however. People, it seems, now have far more options than ever but far less capacity to choose the right one because they know themselves less. The high school student who reaches for the pocket calculator may never know the mathematical flair he or she truly possesses. TV is not just a substitute for creative leisure, a book, a game, a conversation; it is becoming more and more a substitute for thought. Rollo May has said it so well:

We are bombarded with advertising which tells us that a new world lies at the end of every plane ticket and every endowment policy. We are promised every hour on the hour (in the commercial spot) our daily blessing, told of the tremendous power available in the harnessing of our computers, in the techniques of mass communication, in the new electronic age which will re-form our brain waves and make us see and hear in new ways, and in cybernetics, in the guaranteed income, in art for everyone, in new and ever-more amazing forms of automatic education, in LSD which "expands the mind" and releases the tremendous potential that was once hoped for from psychoanalysis but which now—thanks to an accidental discovery—can be achieved much more effortlessly and quickly in drugs, in chemical techniques which remake personality, in the developing of plastic organs which replace worn-out hearts and kidneys and in the discovering of how to prevent nerve fatigue so that one can live on almost indefinitely, and so on ad infinitum. And it is not surprising that the listener is confused at times as to whether *he* is the anointed one, the recipient of all the blessings from these genii or just the dumb fall-guy? And, of course, he is both.[14]

A recent copy of the *Monitor* (a monthly newspaper published by the American Psychological Association) has two articles back-to-back in the same issue. The first article, featured on the cover page, carries the provocative title "Data Smog: Newest Culprit in Brain Drain." The author, Bridget Murray, writes, "According to some psychologists and researchers the 'data smog' that bombards us every day may be making us ill by interfering with our sleep, sabotaging our concentration and undermining our immune system. David

Lewis, Ph.D., a British psychologist calls the malady 'information fatigue syndrome'. The fast flow of facts motivates people to a point, but once it pushes past a critical threshold, their brains rebel."[15]

On the next page the same author writes under the title, "Weave your Own Web Site: An Essential Tool, Resource," "If you've got the time, you can create your own web site for a course, or your psychology department."[16] And so *we must create* the time to establish and use the very technology described as a "culprit" in her first article. It's like a magazine that advertises a diet drink and fudge cake mix on opposite pages.

MORAL REASONING

As technology can reduce the human capacity for responsible decision making it also can reduce the capacity for moral reasoning. As options increase geometrically the time and capacity for evaluating options decreases, as well as reflection on the consequences of choosing one option over another. As choices become increasingly under the control of stimuli and hence more automatic rather than reflective, moral reasoning predictably declines. Judgment takes time as does the consideration of consequences in the moral order of things, however the on-rush of data calls for knee-jerk responses. As responses are less conscious, less considered, and less evaluative there is an accompanying decrement in moral reasoning.

Perhaps the decay in moral judgment as witnessed in our postmodern world is attributable, at least in part, to the rapacious influx of technology into our daily lives—a technology that begs for application before one can realize the full implications of that application.

E-mail and fax technology are an excellent case in point. Both convey the urgency of an immediate response—message begets message. No longer does the recipient of a fax message have the time to consider the merits and implications of a response, but respond you must, and now not later. And once you push the "send" button, there's no retrieving what was said.

Not too many years ago letter-writing involved a four-to-six day cycle and responses (if at all) could readily be extended beyond that time. Important letters were carefully drafted and language selected for its precision in conveying just the right intention and meaning. Often language could be employed to convey a second meaning not found in the words themselves (language is both denotative and connotative). Unfortunately e-mail and fax messages obscure the subtlety of language and can deprive the receiver of the full intention and meaning of the transmittal.

Wireless phones, because of their omnipresence, invite rapid, insensitive and indiscriminate use where feelings and consequences get obscured by the technology itself.

Moral reasoning can be adversely affected by technology in three important ways.

1. Choice shifting

The capacity to reach huge audiences allows marketers to dump their wares on unwary people, forcing them to make choices they would not normally make and are disinclined to make. Telemarketing is a case in point. Dinner can be disturbed by a nameless, faceless voice, sometimes thousands of miles away, compelling you to respond in some fashion to a product or service you never would have considered otherwise. The cluttering of such impersonal information in our lives via internet, telemarketing and other means tends to depreciate the intrinsic value of truthful information and our requirement to show careful judgment, to reflect and act responsibly.

2. Choice blurring

The dizzying array of information presented on TV and computer screens (not to mention telemarketing and mail) confuse the receiver so that information is sorted and combined beyond the brain's capacity for classification and storage. Short-term memory is overworked with combinations of the important and the trivial. Trivial messages can be retained because of their stimulus qualities and important messages can be lost because they lack stimuli which can compete successfully for attention. Good stuff gets unnoticed, useless stuff gets our attention, and we can form judgments based on disconnected and irrelevant information. What is good and what is true are blurred in the process.

3. Automaticity

Technology is inherently fast and getting faster every day. We are bombarded with images and messages with such rapidity that reflection and evaluation have become depreciated as important qualities of human thought. Values have shifted from reflective thought with consideration of consequences to a "just do it" philosophy, whereby consequences can be scuttled by a new set of responses. Those whose minds work slowly and who enjoy reflective thought are a drag in today's rapid-fire world where the need to do more and more negates the human capacity for consideration of the implications of actions and evaluation of consequences—hence a deterioration in moral judgment.

A NEW DIMENSION

Our technical capacity has taken us out of this world and into a new dimension of reality not governed by earth's time and space. We have passed through the merely possible and improbable and are now in the dimension of the once unknowable. Humanity has advanced technology to the point where it is no longer an extension of the person. Humanity has, in a sense, established a new place that exists in the impossible world for which the human person was not created. It took millions of years for the human being to evolve into a land creature, but only a few short years to become a space creature, for which the person has not evolved. When Neil Armstrong stepped onto the moon thirty years ago, he was essentially doing the impossible, from humanity's point of view. Space and the surface of the moon are an alien environment for the human being. Human beings' presence on the moon is entirely of our own doing— not so humanity's presence on earth. Indeed, there is now the idea of "terra-forming," whereby other planets are made to become habitable by forms of life on earth.[17] An International Space Station, begun in November 1998 is now becoming a reality that will involve innumerable space walks during the next several years.

Machines have made it possible for humanity to do the otherwise impossible—to leave or to destroy the very environment that has produced us and that continues to sustain us. And as we have created a new dimension of reality beyond ourselves, we must likewise achieve a new dimension of reality within ourselves. As we extrapolate ourselves out of this space and this time, we must ourselves establish a new territory within. As the possibilities are limitless and infinite without, they must be limitless and infinite within. Blaise Pascal wrote that humanity is a middle point between two infinities—nothingness and infinity beyond the self..[18] The only possible compensation for our relentless search beyond ourselves is an equally relentless search within ourselves. As humanity reaches into the universe beyond, we must reach into the universe within. Aldous Huxley writes about this as a function of education:

Man is a multiple amphibian and exists at one and the same time in a number of universes, dissimilar to the point, very nearly of complete incompatibility. He is at once an animal and a rational intellect; a product of evolution closely related to the apes and a spirit capable of self-transcendence; a sentient being in contact with the bright data of his own nervous system and the physical environment and at the same time the creator of a home-made universe of words and symbols, in which he lives and moves and has anything from thirty to eighty percent of his being. . . . But this world of symbols is only one of the worlds in which human beings do their living and learning. They also inhabit the non-symbolic world of unconceptualized or only slightly conceptualized experience. However effective it may be on the conceptual level, an education that fails to help young amphibians to make the best of the inner and outer universes on the hither side of symbols is an inadequate education.[19]

If behaviorism is correct, if, indeed, behavioristic theory is the most accurate account of human conduct, then certainly its effects must be cumulative. That is, as we continue on this planet, the contingencies in the environment must necessarily become richer, more varied, more subtle, covering an ever-expanding spectrum of human behavior. After all, in responding to the environment, we contribute to the environment, adding thusly to the contingencies available to us and our children. (From times-tables to calculators to computers.) In this way, learning leads to new learning, and knowledge leads to new knowledge. If, indeed, behaviorism is an adequate account of civilization, then humans must necessarily progress from generation to generation with increasing capacity to take on the environment. As humanity ventures forward, previously neutral events suddenly provide positive reinforcement or serve as negative reinforcers. From the point of view of science and technology this is true, but what of art, literature, and culture? How is it that Shakespeare lived 400 years ago? What were the contingencies in Shakespeare's environment that produced his behavior? How, then, Michaelangelo 100 years earlier? Ovid lived 2,000 years ago, Homer 800 years before him. Certainly the reinforcements available to Aristotle were less rich, less varied than today. According to behaviorism, today's culture should show the same advances over the past as technology and science—but this arguably does not appear to be the case. Could there be something within the person that is out of reach of environmental reinforcers, that is beyond the shaping power of environmental contingencies? Is not a human being ultimately a human being, despite the environment?

It is perhaps for this reason that a repeated experience for astronauts who have traveled to the moon is found to be a spiritual one. For some, the trip represented a spiritual transformation, an experience of mystical dimensions, the discovery of Pascal's "middle point." In exploring the universe, we are ultimately confronted with ourselves, which calls for new and perhaps more profound effort. The interior self is perhaps the most elusive territory of all. Scholars love to argue the point, but could this be the territory Huckleberry Finn really had in mind, when in the last lines of Mark Twain's great novel, he says, "I reckon I got to light out for the territory"?

Whether or not we survive, whether or not our humanity passes the test, is a matter of our spirit, our determination, and the power of our will to be, to continue to exist on this planet or on another, in this time or in another. As we have managed to harness energy for our machines, we must likewise manage to harness our own potential as human beings. We must will our own existence. We must create our own destiny. Albert Schweitzer has concluded that there is hope in human nature and human will:

Judging by what I have learned about men and women, I am convinced that there is far more in them of idealist will power than ever comes to the surface of the world. Just as the water of the streams we see is small in amount compared to that which flows underground, so the idealism which becomes visible is small in amount compared with what men and women bear locked in their hearts, unreleased or scarcely released. To unbind what is bound, to bring the underground waters to the surface: mankind is waiting and longing for such as can do that.[20]

THE HUMAN MOTIVE

Our discussion of thematic motivation distinguishes among gratification motivation, actuation motivation, and altruistic motivation. Humanity plots its course. Humans choose to live according to the thematic motive that is regarded as most important. The person indulges the ego, expands the ego, or expends the ego. And we do so freely unless our freedom has been greatly diminished by forces within or outside ourselves.

We know that our will to survive must be exercised through the thematic motivational system. Since survival, purpose, and destiny are existential issues, the thematic motivational system is required to move us forward into a future we create. As we have established earlier in our discussion of the thematic motivational system, it is thematic motivation that marks each person's life as one of desperation or hope. Humanity owns its destiny by virtue of the thematic motives. Neither the formative nor operational systems are consequential as far as human destiny is concerned. Our humanity and our destiny is manifest in our willful acts. The most human motive, therefore, is the one in which the will most freely participates, that calls for the greatest courage and heroism. The toughest motive for us all is the one that we must work hardest to achieve, where we exert "willpower" in the best sense of the word.

In the very best sense we achieve our peak not through Maslow's self-actualization but through self-transformation or, as better expressed by Aldous Huxley, through "self-transcendence." The whole of the self is transcended by becoming not a fulfillment of its own potential but by joining in a new unity. The self is transformed not within the oneness of one's own being but by sharing one's being with others. In this partnership there is a new unity, a new union, a new oneness, a new capacity for creation.

That this transformation may occur is beyond the human being as a "wanting animal" in the Maslow sense or as a pleasure-seeking organism in the Skinnerian or Freudian sense. Transformation is a result of the will, the will not just to endure, not just to fulfill one's personal potential, but the will to become a renewed being. It is experienced in a surrender of the self in the service of others. Albert Schweitzer writes:

That everyone shall exert himself in that state of life in which he is placed, to practice true humanity toward his fellow man, on that depends the future of mankind. Enormous values come to nothing every moment through the missing of opportunities, but values which do get turned into will and deed mean wealth which must not be undervalued.[21]

The will to serve is humanity at its best; it is each person expressing humanity in its best form. It is humanity's highest expression of its freedom, its creativity, and its love. Those territories within!

NOTES

1. Robert P. Cavalier and Richard Wesp, "The Perception of Familiar Objects," paper presented at the conference, *Teaching of Psychology: Ideas and Innovations*, Ellenville, N.Y., 23 March 1995.

2. Robert Cavalier and Richard Wesp, "The Garbage-Can Illusion as a Teaching Demonstration," *Teaching of Psychology* 24 1997: 125–126.

3. The following posters were presented at meetings of the Eastern Psychological Association:

- Robert Cavalier and Richard Wesp, "The Garbage Can Illusion: Its use as a Teaching Demonstration" (Arlington, Va., 17 April 1993).
- Richard Wesp, Robert Cavalier, Melissa Clough, and Jaye Rancourt, "The Function of an Object as a Determinant of Perception of Its Size" (Philadelphia, 30 March 1996).
- Richard Wesp, Robert Cavalier, Karen Hall, and Jennifer Caruso, "Size Judgments of Common Objects Are Distorted in Both Numerical Estimates and Drawings" (Boston, 27 February 1998).

4. Figure 2 shows the famous Müller-Lyer illusion. The top and bottom lines are the same length, although to most people, the bottom line appears longer.

5. Sonnet 65, in Robert O. Ballou, *The Sonnets of William Shakespeare* (New York: Avenel Books, 1961).

6. Jerry A. Fodor, *The Modularity of Mind: An Essay on Faculty Psychology* (Cambridge, Mass.: MIT Press, 1983), 2.

7. Nicolas Berdyaev, *The Meaning of the Creative Act* (New York: Collier Books, 1962), 134–135.

8. Carl Sagan, *The Dragons of Eden* (New York: Ballantine Books, 1977), 127. Carl Sagan argues that humans and other animals are different only by degree and that humans have eliminated other life forms that could have threatened our intellectual superiority. This is an interesting view but escapes the understanding of humankind not only as thinking but as willing. He suggests a new ethics based on the fact that other animals can form abstractions and share the capacity of thought with humans. Again the point is missed that ethics is derived from human freedom and the human being's capacity to form an act of will and intentionality.

9. Bernard J. Baars, *In the Theater of Consciousness* (New York: Oxford University Press, 1997), 131–133.

10. Ibid., 134. Reference is to James Reason, "Lapses of Attention in Everyday Life," in R. Parasuraman and D. R. Davies, eds. *Varieties of Attention* (New York: Academic Press, 1984).

11. Rollo May, *Love and Will* (New York: Dell, 1969), 224.

12. William James, *The Principles of Psychology*, 2 vols. (New York: Dover, 1950), 8.

13. John Searle draws an analogy between a computer and a room where Chinese symbols are stored and then displayed according to a set of rules that provide instructions on which Chinese symbols to use. As an operator in the room, you can follow instructions without ever knowing the meaning of the Chinese symbols. Knowing the meaning of the symbols is what makes thinking human. (See Hergenhahn, 546–547.)

14. Rollo May, *Love and Will*, 183.

15. Bridget Murray, "Data Smog: Newest Culprit in Brain Drain," *American Psychological Association Monitor* (March 1998), 1, 40.

16. Bridget Murray, "Weave Your Own Web Site: An Essential Tool, Resource," *American Psychological Association Monitor* (March 1998), 41.

17. *USA Today*, 28 July 1998, 4D.

18. Blaise Pascal, *Pensées* (London: Penguin Books, 1966), 90.

19. Aldous Huxley, "Education on the Non-Verbal Level," eds. Hung-Min Chian and Abraham H. Maslow, *The Healthy Personality* (New York: D. Van Nostrand, 1977), 138–139, 141.

20. Albert Schweitzer, "I Resolve to Become a Jungle Doctor," Chian and Maslow eds. *The Healthy Personality*, 210.

21. Ibid, 210.

CHAPTER 8

Deciding

In our every deliberation we must consider the impact of our decisions on the next seven generations. The great law of the six nations.

—Iroquois Confederacy

In his book, *The Informed Heart*, Bruno Bettelheim writes,

What happened in the concentration camp suggests that under conditions of extreme deprivation, the influence of the environment over the individual can become total. . . . This was so much so, that whether or not one survived may have depended on one's ability to arrange to preserve some areas of independent action, to keep control of some important aspects of one's life, despite an environment that seemed overwhelming and total. To survive, not as a shadow of the SS but as a man, one had to find some life experience that mattered, over which one was still in command.

This was taught to me by a German political prisoner, a communist worker who then had been at Dachau for four years. I arrived there in a sorry condition because of experiences on the transport. I think that this man, by then an "old" prisoner, decided that, given my condition, the chances of my surviving without help were slim. So when he noticed that I could not swallow food because of physical pain and psychological revulsion, he spoke to me out of his rich experience: "Listen you, make up your mind: do you want to live or do you want to die? If you don't care don't eat the stuff. But if you want to live there's only one way: make up your mind to eat whenever and whatever you can, never mind how disgusting. Whenever you have a chance, defecate, so you'll be sure your body works. And whenever you have a minute, don't blabber, read by yourself, or flop down and sleep." . . . Soon I became convinced of how sound his advice had been. But it took me years to fully grasp its psychological wisdom.

What was implied was the necessity, for survival, to carve out, against the greatest odds, some areas of freedom of action and freedom of thought, however insignificant.[1]

In this account of his survival Bettelheim tells us that his decision to survive was based on those small acts of personal freedom he managed to maintain, those which he carved out "against the greatest odds." We learn here that true life decisions (as opposed to simple choices) are always formed out of freedom. Without freedom, decisions of any consequence become impossible.

DECISION VS. CHOICE

The importance of decision making has been mentioned several times in this book, along with the point that there is an important distinction between a choice and a decision. As stated earlier, animals choose, but people decide. The discussion can be taken a step further as we consider the awesome power and potential consequences of human deciding—a power that grows out of freedom. All of human enterprise, its institutions, its laws, its science, and its art are the result of human deciding. Consider the awesome and irreversible decisions that have been made: Hiroshima, the Holocaust, defoliation, and beyond. You may ask, Were these truly decisions or the irrevocable consequences of advancing technology and overwhelming political and economic forces? Were Hiroshima and Nagasaki necessary? Could we have decided otherwise? Consider important (maybe regrettable decisions) in your own life. Could they have been different? Is there a power we possess that can claim a decision "against the greatest odds," just as Bettelheim did in his decision to survive? In our own life arenas there are odds to overcome. Tough decisions are around the corner for us as individuals and as a nation. Hate killing and starvation—can we decide otherwise? Certainly information, or the lack thereof, judgment, and human propensities are factors in any decision, but there remains that special moment when we must take ownership of the decision to do or not to do. Bad decisions, such as groupthink decisions, can be the result of refusal to take decision ownership by "passing the buck" or allowing group consensus to take over.[2] Bad decisions happen: Pearl Harbor, the Bay of Pigs, the *Challenger* missile. (Incidentally, high-quality decisions are not dependably the result of group consensus. Individual decisions are frequently seen to outstrip in quality decisions made by groups.)

Decisions, unlike choices, are always all or none. A decision always involves only two possibilities, an affirmative one or a negative one. You decide to continue your education or not to do so, to study music or not to study music, to marry or not to marry, to provide care for your parents or not to do so, to join a religion or not to join a religion, to buy a house or not to buy a house. Decisions are creative acts. They always provide you with new directions or new opportunities. Sometimes they fail. School is not always a successful experience, and marriages frequently fail. Many times, hopes and aspirations are trashed. Sometimes information is misleading or our judgement is poor. Some times we overestimate our abilities to make things happen. But even when things do not go as planned or hoped, we can regroup, make changes, and decide anew. Sometimes decisions require courage—sometimes they invite a great deal of personal effort. They are, however, always generative, they always proceed from the self, and they always involve personal change. Even trivial decisions involve change. A decision to put a new roof on one's house involves change in money available for other things. And a new roof is trivial when compared with other life decisions one makes.

If decisions are always generative and directional, how are they different from choices? The words *choice* and *decision* are frequently used interchangeably and mean the same thing as: "I choose to marry" or " I decide to marry." Although this may be the case, nonetheless, there are two different processes that should be considered, semantics notwithstanding. Choosing is a process of selection from several alternatives. For example after *deciding* to go to college, the person *chooses* which college to attend from many possibilities. Which college is chosen is of course important for many reasons, but the decision to attend college in the first place is far more significant. Many students are disappointed with their choice of college and transfer elsewhere, but the decision to achieve a college education remains. Perhaps the student changes her mind and goes to work instead of school. That's OK, but a decision has then been made not to continue education at this time.

The reason why the distinction between choice and decision is so important is because academic psychology has attempted to understand human nature by observing animals make choices in mazes and in cages of various sorts. Such choices are infrahuman. They are not decisions. Animals do not make decisions. Only humans are capable of decision making. If a rat in a Y maze chooses to go left rather than right, there are various environmental and internal factors that can account for this behavior, but this is clearly not a creative decision on the part of the rat. It is merely a choice from a pair of alternatives prescribed by the experimenter. (The consequences such as the presence or absence of food as a reward, are also prescribed by the experimenter.) What we observe in the animal is some kind of instrumental behavior that occurs within the constraints of the experiment, usually to test an experimental hypothesis. The rat would never do this on its own, for its own reasons, or to meet its own life goals. Rats and pigeons don't act creatively or proactively. They don't have life goals in the human sense of the term. They operate out of instincts or learn new behaviors that have been conditioned into them through environmental reinforcers. Skinner taught pigeons to direct the flight of a missile so it would stay on target—but it's seriously doubtful that pigeons would ever do this on their own. Humans do design missiles, however, which are the result of creative decisions. (We have also decided to dismantle warheads in "silos" in various locations throughout the United States—another example of human deciding.)

CHOICE MODELS

All of the models designed by psychologists to account for human decision making involve the identification and weighing of alternative courses of action. Irving Janis and Leon Mann, in their book, *Decision Making*; suggest a five-stage model as follows:

1. Appraising the challenge
2. Surveying alternatives
3. Weighing alternatives
4. Deliberating about commitment
5. Adhering despite negative feedback[3]

They write, "By the end of stage 2, the decision maker has narrowed down his list of alternatives to those that appear to have a good chance of averting the losses . . . without entailing intolerable costs or risks."[4]

This and numerous models like it all see decision making as a process of sorting out alternatives and selecting one alternative over the others, either by a process of elimination based on some kind of cost-risk analysis, or sequentially based on some minimal standard of acceptance—what Herbert Simon has termed *satisficing*.[5]

All of these models are not really decision models; they are choice models. They are models that emphasize selection, not generative outcomes. These models all overlook thematic motivation.

THE ROMANS KNEW

The word *decide* comes from the Latin words *de*, meaning *from* and *caedere* meaning *cut*. However, the Latin translation for the English word *decide* is *constituere* which carries the added meaning "to cause to stand, place or put." The Latin translation for *choose* is *deligere* which means "to select." *Constituere* refers to constructive action, whereas *deligere* means to "pick or select."[6] Clearly, the Romans understood the distinction between deciding and choosing—a distinction which has become blurred in our vernacular usage.

Abraham Maslow also knew the difference between deciding and choosing, although he also confuses the terms:

Let us think of life as a process of choices one after another at each point there is a progression choice and a regression choice. There may be movement toward defense toward safety, toward being afraid; but over on the other side there is the growth choice. To make the growth choice instead of the fear choice a dozen times a day is to move a dozen times a day toward self-actualization. *Self-actualization is an on-going process*; it means making each of many single choices about whether to lie or be honest, whether to steal at a particular point, and it means to make each of these choices as a growth choice. This is movement toward self-actualization.[7]

This is what Bruno Bettelheim did. His *growth choices* constituted his decision to survive "against the greatest odds." Maslow and Bettelheim clearly show the difference between human choosing and human deciding. Maslow uses the word *choice*, but he means *decision*.

In terms of the motivation model developed in this book, choices are part of the operational system, whereas decisions, described by Maslow as growth choices, belong to either the operational or thematic system of motivation. We buy houses and cars and go on vacation in the operational system; we pursue our life goals in the thematic system. There is a huge difference between the two, keeping in mind that not all thematic decisions are "growth choices," nor do they always contribute meaningfully to the life of others.

A CLOSER LOOK AT DECISIONS AND CHOICES

Deciding is different from choosing in several important ways.

1. Decision making, unlike choosing, is a characteristically human activity. Animals are not capable of making decisions. Animals may be able to choose certain paths of action, but only humans are capable of making decisions.

2. Decisions stem from operational and thematic motivation, whereas choices are always operational—never thematic.

3. Decisions are not necessarily information-based. Choices, however, are always made on the basis of sorting out information represented by different alternatives.

4. Decisions are based on intuitive thinking and urges within the self for more completeness, resolution, self-realization, or altruism. Some information is, of course, necessary but secondary to what flows from within. It reminds one of Plato's reminiscence theory of knowledge, whereby sensory experience is secondary to the content of one's own mind. For Plato, "all knowledge is innate and can be attained only through introspection which is the searching of one's inner experiences."[8]

5. Decisions are always generative. They are creations from within the self that introduce new opportunities and consequences into one's world and perhaps the world of others. (Sometimes they are sinister consequences.)

6. Decisions are always made freely—they are never the result of coercion or constraining life circumstances. One can be forced to take an action but never to make a decision. Decisions necessarily flow from personal freedom and are a defining characteristic of a free person.

Choices, on the other hand, can be the result of environmental conditions, habits, prior learning, force, and so on.

7. Decisions are less predictable than choices and are very difficult, if not impossible to measure, since they are frequently non-normative. Individuals often make decisions that are unexpected and opposite to the group norm.

8. Decisions can range from minor to colossal in their consequences for an individual or for a whole people (from a bird house to an A-bomb). It is awesome to consider the consequences that can be unleashed on self and humanity by the human capacity to decide. Human history is replete with examples that have formed history itself. There are no examples of this in the animal kingdom. In this sense, animals have no history.

9. Decisions are inherently ethical. It is the decision moment that changes potency to actuality—an actuality for which the decision maker necessarily assumes responsibility. Choices may or may not be ethical in character. Sometimes we choose a course of action when we really have no alternative. These distinctions are sometimes very difficult to understand, much less to evaluate and judge. Victor Frankl has this to say: "In a word, each man is questioned by life, and he can answer to life by *answering* for his own life; to life he can only respond by being responsible."[9]

10. Decision quality can improve with education, experience, and moral example and instruction. According to Socrates, "When one's conduct is guided by knowledge, it is necessarily moral. For example, if one knows what justice is, one acts justly."[10] For modern society, it is not always clear what justice is, and decision quality can suffer as a result. Again, was Hiroshima necessary?

11. Decisions invest life with meaning and purpose. Decisions that are the expression of thematic motivation bring our ideals and values into real life. Ideals and values, good ones, we hope, are nice, but they must be acted upon. Existential and ontological decisions are humanity's way of creating meaning for self and others. (See pp 111–113.)

12. Decisions always make an assertion or a negation of one of only two possibilities. To do or not to do, to assume action or not to assume action, "to be or not to be." There are no in-betweens when real decisions are made. Vascillation, mediocrity, uncertainty (sometimes even compromise) are not the stuff of good decision making. "He who is not with me is against me" was the way Christ put it.[11] For this reason, tough decisions frequently involve human effort, even courage (the courage of one's convictions), and we are frequently measured by them.

Choices, on the other hand, always involve the assessment, pro and con, of different alternative actions. Not so with decisions. "The fault, dear Brutus, is not in our stars; But in ourselves, that we are underlings."[12]

13. Decisions frequently involve personal confrontation and can produce fundamental change within the person, unlike choices, which often can be used to avoid personal confrontation and maintain the status quo. It is the *deciders*, not the *choosers*, who really create change in their world, for good or for bad.

14. Decisions involve full conscious involvement. They are acts of human willing.

15. Decisions are binding in the sense that they necessarily call for suitable action (or lack of action) against sometimes difficult odds. Choices are more variable. For example, one can shift choices and still remain resolved in one's decision. A constructive life with positive effects on self and others is produced by a series of firm decisions—career, marriage, children, and so on.

GENERATIVITY

True human decisions are always generative. A choice is not generative, a choice is selective—it does not create in and of itself. To choose between a movie or a ball game is not generative, to choose one restaurant over another is not generative, nor is choosing a book, a job, nor even a course of study *necessarily* generative.

Generativity is itself an interesting word. It is certainly a very potent word. Potency and generativity are closely allied, are they not? One must be potent to be generative. Erik Erikson uses the word in describing that stage of development that he calls adulthood. For Erikson, the adult stage of development involves a crisis between generativity and stagnation; a sign of the mature, fully functioning adult is that person's capacity to be generative, to exert influence upon the world and the environment, and the care of future generations.[13] It is in Erikson's use of the term that we see a correlation between the capacity to decide and human maturity. In fact, one could define maturity as the ability to decide. This point will be developed a little later.

A decision then originates within the individual, it is generative, and it flows out of the person into the world. Every human decision begins in potentiality—a potential we all experience by virtue of our freedom. This potential is an almost infinite value limited only by the time and space in which it generates actuality. Actuality necessarily occurs in time and space and is a finite occurrence, one that is observable and measurable and within the reach of science. Potentiality, however, is an infinite reservoir within the person. What this potential, this freedom, becomes in reality, is a function of human decision making, of intending and willing. This willing, this deciding, is a generative act in which we can change the world. We supply the world with objects, with technology, with knowledge and with laws. Generativity, then, is supplying without what begins within—a tool, a work of art, a book, a culture, a civilization, alas, even bombs and wars. All supplied by human deciding, all exteriority of a more potent interiority.

Decisions exist at different levels and are of differing degrees of significance. Decisions range from the *physical*, to the *existential*, to what can be called, for lack of a better word, the *ontological*. All grow out of human motivation. A physical decision concerns some reconfiguration of present time and space. An existential decision concerns a commitment to becoming, a commitment to growth. An ontological decision moves to the transcendent. It is a decision for oneness in being. Decisions therefore vary in depth and psychological meaning. The greater the depth of the decision, the richer the human experience. Physical decisions are rational and cognitive, calling for reasoning and know-how; much of our formal education and training is aimed at physical decision making. An engineer decides to build a bridge; a dentist decides to extract a tooth; a plumber decides to fix a pipe. These are all examples of physical decisions calling for varying levels of knowledge and skill and intelligence. They belong to the operational motivational system, *as does all technology.*

A next level of decision making is existential. To decide to exercise one's potential, to achieve greater personal meaning and purpose, to grow in compassion, in intellect, in aesthetic sensitivity—these are existential decisions and belong to the thematic motivational system.

It is hoped that many of us achieve a level of existential deciding. It is in this area where the so-called "peak experiences" occur.[14] This is the level where the humanists have their field day. This is the level of Abraham Maslow and Carl Rogers and "self-actualization." For the humanist, there is nothing more. To decide to become and to grow is the ultimate personal reality. Rogers says that self-actualization is available to all of us—that we all have this actualizing tendency within us.[15] Maslow describes self-actualization as a process of "growth choices." However, there is a third level of deciding—the ontological level. This is the level of the transcendent, and it is only at this level that an ontological union can occur between self and the universe. This is the ultimate human decision—not becoming, not self-actualization, but transcending time and space. In the spiritual sense it is communion with God. Maslow writes of self-transcendence in his final book, *The Farther Reaches of Human Nature*, but he talks about it as "transcendence of the selfish-self."[16] Maslow's, self-transcendence falls short of self-surrender. It is not the transcendence of Christ or Gandhi or even the transcendence of Schweitzer (Chapter Seven).

Let's go back and retrace some of these ideas more carefully.

Physical decisions result in specific actions that are visible, tangible, and measurable. A decision to build a garage, a fence, or a missile, for that matter, is a physical kind of decision. The project begins at a certain point in time, and ends at a certain point in time. It might take three weeks to build a garage, three years to build a missile. Time and space are involved as well as material and financial resources, all of which—the time, the space and the resources, material and financial—can be measured. All are finite. Perhaps the number is few—perhaps it grows fewer every day—but there probably are people whose decision-making level never gets beyond the physical, who rarely move to the next level of human deciding that can be called the existential level—that level of decision that is less visible, less tangible, less measurable, if at all. Such decisions are decisions centered in human development and becoming—decisions that result in human growth, human fulfillment, human satisfaction, for self *and* for others, for the present *and* for the future. All such decisions are existential and belong to the thematic motivational system. The best existential decisions are those designed to release an inherent power for good in self or in others. Existential decisions actualize human potency and are timeless. To be sure, all events of human experience begin and end in time. However, existential decisions, although finding their beginning in time, themselves have no time limit. The decisions to become educated or to educate, or to enhance the human condition, for example, have no time limit. The decisions of Christ, Gandhi, and Martin Luther King have no time limit. They are truly existential decisions. (Some worry that technology that appears to be instrinsically operational may be eroding this kind of decision making.)

The New York Times gives an account of such a decision in telling the story of the small French town Oradour-Sur-Glane.

All of the town's past was taken away one bright June 10 more than a half-century ago, when the SS came through. As part of a terror campaign to cow the French Resistance, the SS machine-gunned the men, herded women and children into the church and set it alight, then burned the village down.

Nearly everybody in Oradour was killed, 642 people in all, although it was never learned why Oradour had been chosen for the massacre.

The burned remnants of that story, and of Oradour's history, have loomed for 54 years over the reconstructed town. Old metal sewing machines, bicycles, pots and pans, even cars, all grotesquely twisted from the heat, still lie in fragmentary buildings that gape at the sky. Charles de Gaulle himself called Oradour "the symbol of the country's suffering."

The state carefully preserved the crumbling walls, and everyone here knows by heart the meaning of the number 14. That was how many fellow Frenchmen, from Alsace, were later convicted for taking part in the massacre, among 21 in all. Never mind that the Germans forced 13 Alsatians to join the SS and thus participate in the killings. For years townspeople who had Alsatian visitors were scorned. The Strasbourg soccer team was boycotted in nearby Limoges.

But last week for the first time in 54 years an Alsatian walked through the ruins of Oradour openly declaring his origins. The Mayor of Strasbourg, Roland Ries, was invited to [join] in the annual commemorative ceremony of June 10. . . .

Mr. Ries, who proposed the visit, said in an interview, "I said to myself, 54 years later, the time had come for a reconciliation, and to talk to each other, and share the grief of the families."[17]

Such a reconciliation for a whole town is certainly an existential decision, as would be any reconciliation in our own lives.

PEOPLE, NOT PIGEONS

Carl Rogers sees the person as his or her own ultimate resource, and the capability to make a decision and the nature and quality of human deciding makes all the difference. Rogers, Maslow, and others see the importance of viewing life as a growing and becoming process. It is not clear, however, that psychological humanists give as much attention to issues of human altruism as they should, that is, as a dismissal of one's self interests for the interests of others. They seem more concerned with the psychology of growth from within, with self-realization and self-fulfillment. What is important is the interior self, and not the expenditure of self for others.

The third level of decision is called the ontological decision—the decision to achieve oneness in being. It takes many forms. For some it takes the form of religion; for others social justice, for others truth, for others beauty. It is never self-centered. It is *not* self actualization, it is not growth, it is not becoming. It is not what Maslow calls "metamotivation." It is the decision to regard self as a participant, so to speak, in a unifying process that is more than the self. The best modern example, although certainly there are many examples, is Mother Teresa. She said, while being interviewed on the occasion of being awarded the Nobel Peace Prize, that her work in helping the starving people of India was not altruism in the humanitarian sense of doing good for others. Rather, she said, she thought of each person she helped as Jesus Christ. For her, the work was based on an ontological decision. It was not a decision centered in self. Her concern was not self-realization or the actualization of her potential as a person. For her, it was a decision of self for Christ, an intensely spiritual and religious decision— in the ontological sense, a unity with God. Truth, love, social justice—they were all present in her decision.

Allport has expressed his interest in the ontological level of deciding by describing for us the highest level of Hindu motivation—beyond pleasure, power, and duty—in the person's search "for a philosophical or religious meaning."[18]

This ontological decision, then, is a decision centered in the meaning of existence. It is intensely personal and it is intensely private. Its results may be felt by others, but the decision is made alone; it is formulated in the depths of one's consciousness and one's sense of being. It is the most dynamic process of movement from human potency to human act. It is therefore beyond becoming. It is not simply existential. It is of essence rather than of existence.

The human person is human and person and experiences humanity and personhood most essentially when able to make an ontological decision. Truth, justice and beauty are those attributes of being that humanity moves to in the ontological sense. It is a profound undertaking. It is the ultimate search and the ultimate answer. It is the difference between wisdom and knowledge.

Earlier, a definition of maturity was given that said it is the ability to make a decision, as it were—the ability to be generative, to imprint the world in increasingly significant ways as we grow more mature. Our capacity to decide to do, to become, and to be is a direct measure of our maturity as individuals and as a people. To never have resolved the crises of our youth, to be frozen in fear, worry, uncertainty, and self-doubt marks the immature individual. Maturity by this argument, then, is the capacity to decide, to move from the interior to the exterior, to learn, and to do it again and again, ideally at levels of increasing social, intellectual, aesthetic, and spiritual significance.

And so we come to that process we call education. Education happens within the person as each person achieves maturity. Better stated, education is that process whereby the person moves in steady degrees to full maturity, culminating in the awareness and appreciation of one's meaning and purpose. Certainly there is nothing in this definition that suggests any kind of formal process, but neither is it a passive or evolutionary process. Rather it is a process centered in the capacity to decide and the kinds of decisions one makes in life. An uneducated man by one standard can indeed be a very mature person by this standard. It may be what Mark Twain meant when he said that he would "never let his schooling interfere with his education." It is the process of deciding that makes all the difference—the best use of the thematic motivational system.

All education, formal or informal, is aimed at helping people achieve the capacity to decide. Liberal education most especially is the attempt that ideally moves the individual from physical decisions resulting in technology to existential decisions that are centered in human growth and development. Finally and most essentially may education move humanity to love and truth. I would add that this is more the business of psychology than is the "functional analysis of behavior."

People, not pigeons!

NOTES

1. Bruno Bettelheim, *The Informed Heart* (New York: Avon Books, 1960), 147–148.

2. Groupthink is a process researched by Irving Janis at Yale, who discovered that group forces can override critical judgment in making decisions. Such groupthink decisions are frequently faulty as a result. Janis's research has shown that groupthink can produce disastrous results, such as leaving Pearl Harbor vulnerable to Japanese air attack. For a complete discussion of groupthink and its

symptoms, see Irving L. Janis, *Victims of Groupthink* (Boston: Houghton Mifflin, 1972).

3. Irving Janis and Leon Mann, *Decision Making* (New York: Free Press, 1977), 174.

4. Ibid., 173.

5. Herbert A. Simon, *Administrative Behavior: A Study of Decision-Making Processes in Administrative Organizations*, 2d ed. (New York: Macmillan Publishing Co., 1957).

6. Cassell's Latin Dictionary (New York: Funk and Wagnalls Co.).

7. Abraham Maslow, *The Farther Reaches of Human Nature,* 44 (see chap. 5, n. 22).

8. Hergenhahn, 40 (see chap. 3, n. 11).

9. Frankl, 131(see chap. 4, n. 12).

10. Hergenhahn, 36 (see chap. 3, n. 11).

11. Matthew 12:30.

12. *Julius Caesar*, 1.2.140–141 (see chap. 6).

13. Erik Erikson is among several neo-Freudians who reject the determining role of early childhood in molding human personality. He extended Freud's three primary stages (oral, anal, and phallic) to eight stages encompassing the entire life cycle. His concept of generativity characterizes the mature adulthood of the seventh stage of what he terms the "Eight Ages of Man." For a discussion, see Erik H. Erikson, *Childhood and Society* (New York: W. W. Norton & Co., 1963), 247–274.

14. Abraham Maslow, *Toward a Psychology of Being* (see chap. 4, n. 6).

15. Carl Rogers, *On Becoming a Person*, (Boston: Houghton Mifflin Co., 1961).

16. Abraham Maslow, *The Farther Reaches of Human Nature*, 262.

17. Adam Nossiter, "A Wartime Nightmare Is Still Alive in a Small French Town," *New York Times*, 18 June 1998, sec. A, p. 11.

18. Gordon W. Allport, "The Open System in Personality Theory," 304 (see chap. 1 n. 6).

CHAPTER 9

Work and Leaders

The hands themselves *want* to do things and the mind loves to apply itself. . . . Working is its own end and brings its own joy.

—James Hillman, *A Blue Fire* (p. 172)

The reason for a chapter on management in a book on human motivation is to illustrate how the effective application of poor theory has worked in the past to the essential detriment of the American worker. This book is about human motivation as a principle of differentiation, not as a principle of similarity, and one of the ways in which people are differentiated and thereby more adequately understood is in terms of motives, not acts. As has been so frequently stated in this book, the same behavior can be prompted by totally different motives. A worker can perform beautifully because she wants to impress coworkers, needs the added pay, just enjoys doing something right, or feels morally obligated to do her best at all times. The motives are different in every case because the people are different. Management, therefore, that tries to apply a principle "across the board," such as a job enrichment program or group participation in decision making or autonomous work teams, can be sorely off target.

People do indeed differ in so very many ways. They differ in physical and mental capacities, experience, education, values, aspirations, needs, talents, age, sex, and so on. The most important thing for a manager to do is not to search for a panacea, a "psychological truth" that will make things rosy but rather to develop perception, sensitivity, and judgment—to use principles cautiously, never to expect miracles, and to understand that his or her values, motives, leadership style, and even cognitive style, are a part of the total picture. For example, it was seen in research reported at The Conference Board at a meeting with the theme Understanding Managerial Excellence that the leadership style and the cognitive style of managers may have an interactive relationship.[1] Leaders cannot be separated from the work environment, and as such, they must come to appreciate their limitations and strengths. To motivate workers is one of the chief purposes of leaders. No formula is automatic. There are no sure things. What will work in one setting will flop in another, because the people and culture are different. One worker whose father was a strict disciplinarian relates easily to an authoritarian boss or resents taking orders; another worker raised in a highly permissive home feels that the boss is too bossy or not tough enough. The reason for the differences is found in the different formative motivational systems in both cases.

It is also interesting that years (and tons) of research have produced inconclusive results regarding leadership and personality. The perennial question, "Are leaders born or made?" still plagues us today. One opinion is that leadership is situationally determined. That is, whether or not you are a good leader depends less on your inherent attributes than on the mix of your attributes with the situation in that you are asked to lead. Some authors have identified different situational variables which call for different leadership styles.[2]

Years ago, leaders were looked at in terms of personality traits. It was thought initially that if there are such things as good leaders, they must possess certain characteristic traits. Personality traits, after all, were relatively stable and, therefore, would carry over from situation to situation. If it were possible to identify those traits that characterized effective leaders, then through psychological testing it would be possible to identify young people who, possessing those traits, would eventually become good leaders. The argument seemed plausible enough, but research failed to demonstrate any dependable relationship between personality and leadership. The conclusion, therefore, was that leadership is determined by other factors; this had to be the case if personality traits could not be found that were consistent from leader to leader. The fact that Vince Lombardi was a great coach with St. Cecilia High School, Fordham University, West Point, the New York Giants, the Green Bay Packers, and the Washington Redskins is irrelevant or probably because of similar features in the environment! Nonsense. Lombardi would have been a great leader in a multitude of situations, but not because of his personality traits. The question of personality traits and leadership is simply the wrong question. The right question asks if there is a correlation between motivation and leadership, not personality and leadership. Is the leader motivated to do those things, that will produce desired results? Is he motivated to motivate others? Is he motivated to get the job done even against great odds? What, indeed, are the relationships among formative, operational, and thematic motivation and successful leadership?

As has been stated over and over again in this book, others can be understood best in terms of motives, not personality, not situation, but motivation. Management has begun to understand that motivation is a complex human variable that calls for flexibility and variability and that it is motivation that underlies effective management decisions. Motives result in decisions, personality traits notwithstanding. If, for example, there is dissension between management and workers, and management or workers *decide* to take constructive action, then things can improve, but not until a decision is made to do so. Motives need to be examined. If in the case of conflict the workers' motives are to undo the leader or vice versa, certain behavior will occur. If, however the leader and workers decide to take constructive, rather than destructive, action, then the chances for improved relations becomes much better. Motivation provides the key to successful leader-worker relationships.

The story of motivation and management is an interesting and somewhat sad tale. Despite unprecedented strides in industrial technology, American managers were "blockheads" when it came to psychological principles of human motivation. Perhaps for very good reasons there was a natural resistance to ivory tower "eggheads." "Blockheads and eggheads"——who was to win? Well, it was not until the Hawthorne experiments of 1924 that management gained any insight into the motivations of industrial workers. The Protestant ethic, which says that work, while onerous, was also a source of blessing, had a viselike grip on management thinking for hundreds of years. To work is a human duty, and to accept one's obligation dutifully and without complaint is a sign of true character. Individuals become the spiritually elect through faith, religious devotion, and personal responsibility. So work was seen as a necessary condition of life—as an opportunity to demonstrate responsibility.

Work was sudorific. Human beings were somehow purified by their own sweat. Management just assumed, therefore, that people would find work to be onerous but necessary. It followed that repugnant conditions of work, whether real or perceived, were the natural consequences of life, and so for many years the thoughts and theories of psychologists never impacted management thinking and decision making. Psychology was OK for academics and counselors, but not for managers and workers. Fanciful formulations regarding human aspirations and satisfactions were not necessary when it came to managers, for the management job was a simple one: reward good workers with more money and better positions and punish bad workers by denying increases, promotions, or further training. Since work was inherently distasteful, the only possible way to get people to perform was to threaten them by cutbacks and firings and reward them with larger paychecks and better benefits. Unionism, of course, assumed the same philosophy: reduce the unpleasantness of work and increase the tangible rewards.

The good manager, by this definition, was the one who maintained productivity at minimum expense. Good managers did not have to know psychology, they had to know people, and people behaved the same when it came to work.

That is, they would do as little as possible without jeopardizing position or pay. Exceptional workers on the other hand, rose to the surface and were promoted.

Scientific management, a somewhat inaccurate term for mechanistic management, at the beginning of this century inadvertently took the dehumanization of American workers one step further. According to scientific management theorists, notably the efficiency pioneers Frederick W. Taylor and Frank and Lillian Gilbreth, the human being could be seen as a sort of organic machine with measurable capacities and tolerances. People could stretch, bend, lift, and pull with predictable skill and force under measurable conditions of stress. According to Taylor, an optimal level of efficiency existed when the worker and the physical work environment were in harmonious relationship. In this special sense, the worker was not a human being with will and effort, but a movable and moving object with a built-in design that, like a machine, could perform certain operations much more effectively than others. In this regard, it was not the human but the infrahuman attributes of the worker that were all-important. The only awkward aspect of their theory was the damning fact of individual differences. Not all workers were the same in size, shape, age, stamina, and so on. Some were tall, some short, some strong, some weak, some tired easily; there were those whose reach was too long and others whose reach was too short. Individual differences were not an advantage but a distinct disadvantage in designing the workplace and the operation to be performed. Also, peculiarly, some people were able to produce more than others. Those individual differences! Some also were simply lazier than others. Undaunted, Frederick Taylor developed another surefire method—the incentive system. "Taylor, always the Puritan, proposed that a system of financial incentives be used, in which each worker was paid in direct proportion to how much he produced rather than simply according to a basic hourly wage. An incentive plan thus served much the same purpose in Taylor's organization theory as did the discipline, dogma, and threats of earlier, military, religious, and feudal managers."[3] If you pay more to workers who produce more, you not only make wages a function of production, you also get people to work harder, thus producing more goods in a shorter period of time. This provided you with a distinct pricing advantage over your competition. Everyone was happy, the owners realized a greater margin of profit, the managers got out more goods, and the workers brought home more pay. Those workers who couldn't "hang in there" either quit or were laid off—and good riddance, too. Damn those individual differences! Turnover was costly, but unavoidable to maintain standards and to eliminate those workers who could not hold up their end.

Did scientific management work? Yes, but not because it was "scientific." It worked because the economics of the time allowed it to work and because as a system it was congruent with prevailing management philosophy. And so the system continued through the '20s and into the Depression. Also, it is clear why unionism grew into such massive proportions. (We must not forget that unionism subscribed to the same ethic that characterized management thought.

Unions were not involved in making work more meaningful for the worker, rather, the concern was making work less onerous, less hazardous, less menial and achieving certain guarantees in terms of security and pay.)

HAWTHORNE AND AFTER

In 1924 at the Hawthorne Plant of the Western Electric Corporation, a project was instituted to investigate the effects of the work environment on productivity.

Called the Hawthorne Studies, these research programs took industrial psychology beyond the selection and placement of workers to the more complex problems of human relations, morale, and motivation.

The research began as a reasonably straightforward investigation of the effects of the physical aspects of the work environment on worker efficiency. The researchers asked such questions as: What is the effect on production of an increase in the level of illumination? Do temperature and humidity affect production? What happens if rest periods are introduced?

The results of the Hawthorne studies were astounding to both the investigators and the Hawthorne plant managers. It was found that social and psychological conditions of the work environment were of potentially greater importance than the physical work conditions. For example, changing the level of illumination from very bright to nearly dark did not diminish the level of efficiency of a group of workers. Other, more subtle, factors were operating to cause these workers to maintain their original production levels under almost dark conditions.

In another case, illumination was increased and production levels rose. Other changes were then introduced - rest periods, free lunches, a shorter workday - and with the introduction of each change, production increased. But the most startling result occurred when all the improvements were eliminated: production still increased! It was concluded that the physical aspects of the work environment were not as important as had been supposed.[4]

The Hawthorne studies have achieved the status of classical research on human motivation, for it was discovered that many motives besides pay and physical working conditions operated in the workplace. It was shown that workers could be productive out of a sense of personal importance; that productivity could be increased under conditions of fair play, and that an opportunity to socialize on the job, even a little, could pay off in greater productivity. The Hawthorne results were really quite remarkable, and can be credited with instituting a new era in management thinking—a point of view that reached its peak in the human relations movement of the '50s.

Armed with the results of the Hawthorne experiments, a new field of applied psychology began to take shape. This new field, known initially as personnel psychology, then industrial psychology, and today as industrial/organizational psychology, has grown rapidly since World War II. Division 14 of the American Psychological Association is the Division of Industrial and Organizational

Psychology. Today it is more fashionable to emphasize organizational psychology, because it is more reflective of cultural and social dynamics inherent in organizational life, and therefore, more directly related to issues of human satisfaction and creativity than fields of industrial psychology which include personnel selection, testing, training, performance evaluation, and so on.

Management turned to four theorists as the gurus of a whole new school of thought on industrial motivation.   These theorists were Abraham Maslow, Douglas McGregor, Frederick Herzberg, and David McClelland. Perhaps the most important single contributor was Douglas McGregor whose book *The Human Side of Enterprise* was published in 1960. Heavily influenced by the earlier writings of Maslow, McGregor reconceptualized Maslow's theory of motivation in the context of industrial enterprise.[5] You will recall from Chapter Five that Maslow's theory was based on a hierarchy of human needs: (1) physiological, (2) safety, (3) love, (4) esteem, and (5) self-actualization.

McGregor pointed to the love, esteem, and self-actualization needs as those directly influenced by management policies and methods. McGregor said that workers on the job have a strong need for acceptance and belonging—that they want to feel that they are a part of things. If this is true, argued McGregor, it becomes incumbent upon management to recognize the simple social elements that exist in work and to organize these elements to allow the belonging need to be satisfied. This meant that management should permit social interaction and encourage team effort.

This, of course, was entirely consistent with the enlightened view of the times: man was more than a machine, more than simply a reacting organism. Man was a social being with compelling social drives and desires for interaction, belonging, and love—to love and be loved. David McClelland refers to this as the need for affiliation. Further, management could also do a lot to help workers satisfy their need for esteem. According to Maslow, there are two kinds of esteem need: a sense of personal competency and recognition for accomplishment. Certainly, management could design jobs so that workers would have to exercise their best abilities—to achieve a sense of competence through achievement, and in that process, gain personal recognition for this achievement. The more challenging and more rewarding the work, of course, the greater would be the source of self-fulfillment in work.

McGregor articulated two opposing views regarding human nature and work; he called them Theory X and Theory Y. According to McGregor's Theory X, human nature is perceived as naturally incompatible with work. Theory X makes the following assumptions about human nature:

1) *The average human being has an inherent dislike for work and will avoid it if he can.*

2) *Because of this human characteristic of dislike of work, most people must be coerced, controlled, directed, threatened with punishment to get them to put forth adequate effort toward the achievement of organizational objectives.*

3) *The average human being prefers to be directed, wishes to avoid responsibility, has relatively little ambition, and wants security above all.*[6]

McGregor's Theory Y views human nature as essentially compatible with work. According to Theory Y:

1) *The expenditure of physical and mental effort in work is as natural as play or rest. . . .*

2) *External control and threat of punishment are not the only means for bringing about effort toward organizational objectives. Man will exercise self-control in the service of objectives to which he is committed.*

3) *Commitment to objectives is a function of the rewards associated with their achievement. The most significant of such rewards, e.g. the satisfaction of ego and self-actualization needs, can be direct products of effort directed toward organizational objectives.*

4) *The average human being learns, under proper conditions, not only to accept but to seek responsibility.*

5) *The capacity to exercise a relatively high degree of imagination, ingenuity, and creativity in the solution of organizational problems is widely, not narrowly, distributed in the population.*

6) *Under the conditions of modern industrial life, the intellectual potentialities of the average human being are only partially utilized.*[7]

In this dichotomy between the two conceptions of human nature, McGregor draws the comparison very clearly between the manager who sees workers as people who need to be coerced to perform, and the manager who views people as capable of high performance when the work itself provides satisfaction of human needs.

And so it took McGregor to sum up in clear perspective how the worker could be viewed: as performer or drone. Before this book was written, there was already a prevalent opinion among psychologists and human relations "experts" that social and existential principles operated in the highly motivated person. After all, Maslow wrought his theory twenty years earlier, and Carl Rogers had already been identified as the father of a new movement called person-centered therapy. The role of McGregor's book was to make the facts embarrassingly clear to managers themselves, with the credentials of MIT to boot. Take your pick—Theory X or Theory Y—and how consistent are you? Somehow the whole mess seemed to make sense in a way it never had before. Prior to that time, there had not been as articulate or as convincing a spokesperson for the "human relations cause" as McGregor himself.

CAN WORK BE MOTIVATING?

David McClelland's research at Harvard paralleled the work of Maslow and McGregor, but his work was not explicitly related to management so much as it was to the larger society and culture.[8] McClelland's contribution was seen primarily in what he called man's social needs—the needs for affiliation, achievement, and power.

Although conceived independently in the experimental/clinical tradition, McClelland's work led to a comparable conclusion about human nature—that humans are socially oriented, that they require attention and affection on the one hand, and recognition and power on the other. The important point is that people require internal as well as external motivation. For example, people high in *achievement motivation* must feel a sense of independent responsibility for their actions, strive for recognition by taking calculated risks (calculated to provide positive reactions from others while reducing the possibility of failure) and, therefore, enjoy work that provides feedback on results. Theory X, which sees human nature as naturally indolent, is incompatible with McClelland's achievement motivation. McGregor's Theory Y, however, is much more to the point. Workers simply had to be rescued from the clutches of Theory X managers. After all, we finally have the answer, an answer known to psychologists years before, but now finally accepted, even welcomed, by an enlightened management. Finally, managers knew how to motivate people—make work inherently satisfying.

Herzberg's two-factor theory of motivation was next. Herzberg's theory takes internal motivation an important step forward. His theory contends that an important distinction needs to be made between hygiene factors and motivator factors.[9] Herzberg argued that motivation is an internal process that is generated within the individual by work that is inherently meaningful and intriguing—work that provides an opportunity to experience challenge, creativity, and the satisfaction that comes with commitment and learning. Herzberg claimed that jobs could be enriched in certain ways to make them more rewarding and satisfying to the individual. This theory of individual motivation views satisfaction as the result of rewarding internal processes such as independence, responsibility, and ingenuity. The opposite of satisfaction, according to Herzberg, is lack of satisfaction, not dissatisfaction. The motivated worker is by definition, therefore, a satisfied worker because he finds work a rewarding, even an enriching experience. But a worker can lack satisfaction on the job and still not experience dissatisfaction, provided he is sustained by hygiene factors. Hygiene factors are externals such as salary, benefits, type of supervision, and coworkers. According to Herzberg, hygiene factors are not motivators. They simply prevent dissatisfaction. Money, therefore, is an important hygiene factor in the sense that a good salary can prevent dissatisfaction, but it is clearly not a motivator because it is not intrinsically tied to the job itself. It is an external, not an internal factor. It does not in itself motivate or provide satisfaction.

Research conducted by Herzberg and others would seem to support this conclusion. Surveys on job satisfaction consistently show money down the list below such job elements as opportunity to learn, independent responsibility, and challenging work. Consultants to industry also report similar findings. Money is never ranked as high as internal job elements. Money, it would seem, is not as "satisfying" as challenging work.

The motivational theories of McGregor, Herzberg, McClelland, and others have been extremely useful in understanding the dynamics of human performance at work. The idea of self-enhancement (Maslow's self-actualization, McGregor's self-fulfillment, and Herzberg's satisfiers) have helped managers relinquish their hard-boiled, bottom-line approach (Theory X) and allowed them to see the value in Japanese quality and team-centered approaches to industrial leadership. It took about ten years for their new management philosophy (really McGregor's Theory Y) to settle in, but by the mid-'80s the quality movement finally began to grab hold in this country. (It was around this time that the author conducted sabbatical research at The Conference Board on major management decisions. One decision investigated was the Westinghouse decision to shift from an industrial relations to a human resources management system. Those executives interviewed frequently referred to Japanese productive efficiency— low rejection rates and minimal inventory—based on quality approaches, including quality circles that soon were being used extensively by Westinghouse and other major corporations. In 1984–85, 30 senior officers of several major corporations were interviewed, and the term "total quality" was never used. By 1990, total quality management (TQM) became the most important new method in management thinking since Henry Ford introduced the assembly line. It is still with us and continues to grow in importance, although some of the hoopla has diminished. Work teams have assumed enormous importance in recent years, and reengineering designed around *process teams* has been the latest in bold approaches to undoing traditional hierarchical structures and indigenous management thinking.

All of these developments notwithstanding, motivation in the workplace continues to be a matter of great concern for managers whose competitive environment is more stressful than it has ever been. Technology, globalization, and workforce diversity have changed the workplace forever. Downsizing and numerous mergers representing different organizational cultures have combined to make today's work world vastly different from even a generation ago.

An integrated systems view of motivation can provide a fresh look into workplace dynamics and human performance, since motivational theories of the past have succeeded in obscuring the distinction among formative, operational, and thematic motivation.

DESIGNED FOR LEADERS

Whether it be behavioral, existential, cognitive, or whatever, human motivation is a complex, changeable, and dynamic phenomenon that requires management perception, sensitivity, and judgment. This is especially true in the globally competitive marketplace of today's economy. An integrative-systems theory of motivation therefore is far more realistic and far more useful to managers than is any other theory. Because it is a differential theory of motivation and integrates human differences into an organized view, it is eminently practical for the industrial manager. According to this view, people differ by virtue of their motivation as much as by any other dynamic, whether it be heredity, growth, or learning. Management first and foremost must recognize that people are motivated in different ways. Begin with an attitude of understanding, and establish an opportunity for communication.

It should be remembered that at any point in time, three independent and autonomous motivational systems can be functioning within the individual. What prompts a person to take a certain action or make a certain decision is necessarily a function of one or more of the three systems in an interacting relationship. Actions taken or decisions made at work are especially interesting to evaluate in light of the relative influence of these three systems.

The Formative Motivational System

The Formative System underlies the issues of cultural diversity and individual differences and as such needs to be looked at very critically. The recent merger of Chrysler and Daimler-Benz points to the importance of formative motivation as two well-established organizational cultures need to blend into an effective new enterprise. Formative motivation is past, but its effects are present. This is true for cultures as well as individuals. What does management do to mold a new culture and count on coordinated performance from individuals of different backgrounds? Good communication, sensitivity, and judgment are essential. Mutual respect, expectations, and eventual coordination require anticipating differences from a knowledge of formative cultural differences. Additionally, and most important to realize, is that thematic motivation can override the influence of formative motivation (remember Angela the violinist in Chapter Two). As workers acquire a new vision of the future and are inspired by new challenges and opportunities, new values and belief systems begin to take shape, and behaviors appropriate to these values and beliefs begin to occur. But effective, visionary leadership, centered in confidence, trust, and respect for individual differences, is essential. Leadership makes the difference in producing what I will call "thematic unity." One of the new values in this unity, however, should be a continuing regard for cultural and individual differences and their contributions to effective enterprise.

The Operational Motivational System

Before beginning this discussion, it is useful to refer to the work of Amitai Etzioni and Bernard Bass, who provide two mutually corroborative theoretical viewpoints.

Etzioni has described different kinds of organizational involvement (com-
pliance) that relate to the current discussion.[10]

Etzioni . . . . distinguishes three types of involvement of organization members, as follows: (1) alienative, which means that the person is not psychologically involved but is
coerced to remain as a member; (2) calculative, which means that the person is involved
to the extent of doing a "fair day's work for a fair day's pay"; and (3) moral, which means
that the person *intrinsically* values the mission of the organization and his or her job, and
is personally involved and identified with the organization.[11]

Etzioni's notion of calculative and moral involvement parallel nicely the
operational and thematic motivational systems discussed thus far.

Bass has accumulated extensive evidence from different cultures that distinguishes between transactional and transformational leadership.

Evidence supporting the transactional-transformational leadership paradigm has been
gathered from all continents except Antarctica—even offshore in the North Sea. The
transactional-transformational paradigm views leadership as either a matter of contingent
reinforcement of followers by a transactional leader or moving followers beyond self
interests for the good of the group, organization, or society by a transformational leader.[12]

Bernard Bass describes the transactional leaders as those who, using contingent
rewards, "engage in a constructive path—goal transaction of reward for performance. They clarify expectations, exchange promises and resources for support of the leaders, arrange mutually satisfactory agreements, negotiate for resources, exchange assistance for effort, and provide commendations for successful follower performance."[13]

According to Bass, "Authentic transformational leaders motivate followers
to work for transcendental goals that go beyond immediate self-interests. What
is right and good to do becomes important. [They] motivate followers . . . to do
more than they originally expected to do as they strive for higher order outcomes."[14]

Transactional leaders create operationally motivated people who seek personal and tangible benefits for their efforts; transformational leaders, on the
other hand, provide inspiration to thematically motivated people who are concerned with life ideals and doing what is "right and good" for "the group, organization or country."[15]

The world of work is largely defined by the operational motivational system
involving transactional leaders who use contingent rewards with their followers.
We are a practical people who live in the real world of producing results. Our
approach is pragmatic and utilitarian; we'll work very hard but want to see tangible rewards for our efforts. We are characterized by achievement motivation and
will take calculated risks as the situation demands to achieve our objectives. All

around us we see visible testimony to our ingenuity and persistence. We are, in short, operationally motivated, and our success depends upon our effectiveness in getting the job done. Employers use various employee evaluation systems to help employees identify and achieve their goals. In this process, as Etzioni and McClelland suggest, we calculate how much effort may be necessary to achieve the results we want and adjust our effort based on experience. If further training is necessary, that's OK, provided it will put us on the right track.

The operational motivation system is information, and outcome, centered. Actions are taken and decisions made based on information available and useful to the worker. Management can sustain worker motivation by clarifying goals, stating expectations, providing information, supplying resources, measuring results and providing commensurate recognition and rewards.

Bernard Bass has reported on transaction leaders who get the job done through the use of contingent rewards; in other words, they execute transactions with followers that are nonambiguous and directive. The nature of these transactions are governed by mutual needs and desired results and are contingent ultimately on performance. Workers who are operationally motivated will calculate what they are willing to give based on the perceived value of these transactions. This is as true today as it ever was.

The Thematic Motivational System

Production, marketing, sales, revenue, expenses, and profit are all operationally defined and respond to traditional transactional leadership. We have learned in recent years, however, that this kind of "bottom-line" approach is less able to deal with massive shifts that have occurred in the workplace and in the marketplace. There has been the realization that worker contributions can transcend organizational charts and job descriptions—that worker empowerment is a positive force in maintaining productivity, increasing efficiency, and staying competitive. Leadership today that focuses solely on the operational motivational system is limited in what it can accomplish. The total quality movement has revised organizational values and has called for a new kind of visionary, value-centered leadership, so-called transformational leadership. Bass has provided an excellent account of transformational leadership.

The transformational components are as follows:

Idealized Influence (charisma). Leaders display conviction; emphasize trust . . and emphasize the importance of purpose, commitment, and ethical consequences of decisions.

Inspirational Motivation. Leaders articulate an appealing vision of the future . . . talk optimistically with enthusiasm, and provide encouragement and meaning for what needs to be done.

Intellectual Stimulation. Leaders question old assumptions, traditions, and beliefs; stimulate in others new perspectives and ways of doing things; and encourage the expression of ideas and reasons.

Individualized Consideration. Leaders deal with others as *individuals*[italics
  mine]; consider their individual needs, abilities, and aspirations; listen attentively, further their development; advise; teach; and coach.[16]

Thematic motivation is generated by the transformational components. Any
one of us who has been inspired to do those things that are beyond the "call for
duty" or above self-interests know intuitively what transformational leadership is
and how it differs from the "management" approach of transactional leaders. We
know also how thematic motivation as found in the commitment of today's workers impacts the bottom-line. Larry Hirschhorn in his book *Reworking Authority*
writes:

As firms enter a post-industrial economy, they must indeed remake themselves—inherited career ladders, skills profiles, and the management of information must all change
dramatically. To thrive firms cannot only cut costs. . . . They must also develop new
sources of revenue. For this latter reason they will come to depend increasingly on employees' commitment and creativity. When a company faces this moment in its development, it must in one way or another confront the challenge of building a culture of greater
openness—not, as some gurus would promise, because executives want to humanize their
companies, but because it is the most practical alternative.[17]

MOTIVATING DIFFERENCES

If individual motivation is so complex, how is it possible to lead others at
all? A fair question! A fair answer would be to say that it is most difficult, as
many leaders will attest. Leaders vary—some are transactional, others are transformational; some are authoritarian, others are democratic, some are holistic
intuitive thinkers, others are analytical and logical. Leaders, moreover, have to
produce results that are demonstrable, highly visible, and frequently very difficult to achieve even under the most optimal circumstances. Leaders need people
to get the job done. Moreover, they need people whose motivation, in the Herzberg sense, is generated from within. They also need creative people, people
with good ideas and the guts to express them and argue their point. For the
smart leader, the successful management of individual differences is a most
powerful tactical ability and it is through individual differences, varying views
and ideas, that creative enterprise is launched. Therefore, the good leader must
learn to manage individual differences. When one does, assuming the needed
talent exists, one will succeed.

As was mentioned above, the management of individual differences begins
with an attitude of understanding—in the most legitimate sense, it means the
manager's earnest attempt to understand workers—to understand them as unique
individuals with unique needs, talents, and aspirations. As Allport has said,
"Each person is an idiom." To do this, the manager doesn't treat *everyone the
same*. The manager treats everyone with the same degree of concern and fairness, but this does not mean that everyone is treated as though they were the
same. As a matter of fact, the leader avoids doing so. A capable leader under-

stands that individual and cultural differences are part of each person's formative motivation that is no longer directly accessible. Therefore, leaders should take time—considerable time—in getting to know their subordinates. They must recognize that it *will* take time and therefore requires the right attitude. Good leaders believe in two-way communication and will work hard to create an atmosphere where people are willing to express different and even opposing views to them and to others. They work very hard at communication, and not in the phony sense by calling needless meetings and crafting endless memos or e-mail. They get to know people as people. They learn to enjoy knowing people and establishing trustworthy relationships. They listen, they pay attention, they build confidence. They believe in the potency of communication and in the potency of the individual with whom they communicate. By so doing, they create a climate of openness whereby several things are accomplished: (1) they get to know their people and their abilities; (2) they establish trust whereby people will come to them to express difficulties and concerns; (3) they release creative individuality in their workers; (4) they can initiate and express their own views without creating the impression that they are overpowering others; and (5) they build leadership in followers.

Hirschhorn proposes a similar view. He writes:

Thus to create a culture of openness, organizations must first and foremost build new relationships to authority. Leaders must make themselves more vulnerable to their peers and their subordinates. They must risk their *apparent authority* (the authority that announces they are in charge) in the interest of deepening their substantive authority (the authority they gain from leading a successful team performance.) Followers, for their part, must overcome both their excessive dependence on authority and their blanket hostility to it. In both challenging and accepting, one learns to lead as a follower.[18]

Organizations need to be designed so that optimal interaction among managers and workers can be achieved. Managers must do their utmost to get to know their people. If one finds it is impossible because of the nature of the tasks or numbers involved, one should call for a redesign of the organization into work groups so that communication is tightened without necessarily interposing additional levels of authority. Some organizations have successfully reengineered themselves to accomplish this and to eliminate redundancy of effort. Through various strategies, work can be channeled to the most capable groups of people, to task forces and committees, or to process teams. Through the effective use of assistant coaches and special team assignments, a football coach can get to know all players on the team quite well. Classroom teachers can accomplish the same thing by team teaching and by reorganizing the class into study groups and distributing teaching time from group to group. In this way, it is surprising how teachers can get to know each student quickly and well, whereas this could never be accomplished by lecturing to the whole group all of the time. Team teaching can be very effective in strengthening communication, as is cooperative education whereby students take responsibility for each other's learning.

Each person in a work group has a somewhat different view of a project or an assignment. Rarely will two people see a task in exactly the same way since individual backgrounds, skills, and interests are at play. An effective manager like an effective teacher, utilizes these differences in a creative and meaningful way. If an atmosphere has been created in which people feel free to express their ideas without fear of criticism, the chances improve that innovative solutions can occur. Everyone prizes *individuality* as well as membership on a team. The good manager understands this and uses it. We know that sometimes workers who have experienced tough-minded, do-it-or-else leadership can experience a sense of helplessness, even apathy. This important point is developed in the article: *Combating Organizationally Induced Helplessness*. "An unwillingness by managers to empower their employees often results in learned helplessness in organizations just as perceived loss of power results in learned helplessness in individuals."[19] The empowering manager can help workers overcome their sense of helplessness by encouraging individual and team enterprise as the situation demands.

From the point of view of productivity, effective managers must themselves be operational. They must be able to "size up" a situation and act upon it. They must be critical and objective. Most of all, they must be aware of their own biases and gaps in knowledge, so they can achieve the right attitude and acquire the right information to act operationally and do things for the right reasons.

Today's manager can and should use groups effectively for many reasons, but always *in the service of individual motivation*, not as a substitute for it. This means that today's managers must spend time learning about the people who work for them and relating to them one-on-one, as well as through possible process teams or task forces where there is a chance to "sit in." As managers make an effort to know and relate, they communicate to the worker that they are interested in them as individuals with abilities and ideas. No group can make a person feel or respond better than her boss taking a personal interest in a sincere attempt to utilize her talents, and, by so doing, provide an opportunity for growth. It is certainly a way to overcome a person's sense of helplessness. The key is sincerity and authenticity. This begins in a proper attitude and in a commitment of personal time and energy. Managers who are unwilling to do this have used the work group as a "cop-out" to real human relations. We know also that reengineered organizations can fail where time and commitment are lacking.

Good managers must know their people, their formative, operational and thematic motives. In this way, they can make appropriate assignments, channel tasks effectively, help build work teams in which members' talents are compatible and complementary, and so on. Also, and certainly equally important for the organization, such managers will be able to identify needed areas of skill and knowledge, what training programs are required, and who will profit most from particular developmental experiences or team assignments.

Practically all of what we do at work is operationally motivated and therefore, requires transactional leadership. Good managers must be good transactional leaders in providing direction, clarification, support, reinforcement, and resolving conflicts for the individual and the team. Good managers instill trust and confidence.

Transactional leadership, however, although essential to get the job done on a day-in, day-out basis, should be enlivened by transformational leadership to gain employee loyalty and commitment to the purposes and values of the organization and to a vision beyond day-to-day operations.

FOLLOWERS

There is increasing interest today in the role of the leader in creating an organizational culture where followers emerge as self-leaders. Leaders who are able to produce self-leadership in followers are known today as "super-leaders" because they serve as models for others and motivate others to assume self-leadership.[20] In helping followers assert themselves as individuals and to establish "self-set goals", super-leaders intuitively appreciate the workings of formative, operational and thematic motivation systems that dynamically comprise the self in each follower.

Leaders today, whether viewed as transformational leaders, transactional leaders or as super-leaders clearly espouse the importance of both social forces (followership) and factual data (technology) inherent in the decision making process. The leaders' ideas are crucial but so are the follower's ideas. Opinions and facts intertwine in the decision process which means that social and cognitive elements are present in most decisions. The social and informational components of corporate decisions was anticipated several years ago at The Conference Board research mentioned at the beginning of this chapter. A discussion of this earlier research is provided in the Appendix.

MORAL AUTHORITY

As authority increases in the organizational structure, the emphasis should shift from transactional to transformational forms of leadership. At the highest levels, leadership should be almost entirely transformational. It is the CEO who provides a sense of vision and mission, who is chiefly responsible for instilling new values into the organizational culture, and who also must possess the higher values of integrity, honesty, and trustworthiness.

It is for this reason that the Nixon and Clinton presidencies have been seriously faulted. Both men had superb political and transactional skills, but they have left the country bereft of the transformational leadership every nation requires. As a people, we must go beyond operational motivation. We have advanced as a society and as a nation, not simply because we are an industrious and hard working people, but more importantly, because we have been committed to the values and principles that have been instilled into our nation by its founding assemblies and doctrines. Leadership, especially moral leadership, is of the utmost importance in a free society.

Research has shown that managers who are considerate of workers when making decisions or initiating actions have greater latitude and freedom to make decisions and initiate change. Thus an interactive systems approach to understanding human motivation should be very useful to today's manager. Where there is honesty, trust and understanding, productivity and creativity naturally follow. This is the optimal condition for group and individual enterprise.

NOTES

1. Robert P. Cavalier, Daniel J. Isenberg, Robert Sternberg, and Siegried Streufert, "Understanding Managerial Excellence," presentation given at The Conference Board in New York City, 6 May 1986. Research which I reported at The Conference Board was based on interviews with the senior officers of seven major corporations and revealed the interactive effects of leadership style and cognitive style. Managers who assume different leadership styles, such as unilateral, consultative, or participative, may perform differently because they think differently. These results are described in the following chart:

Figure 3

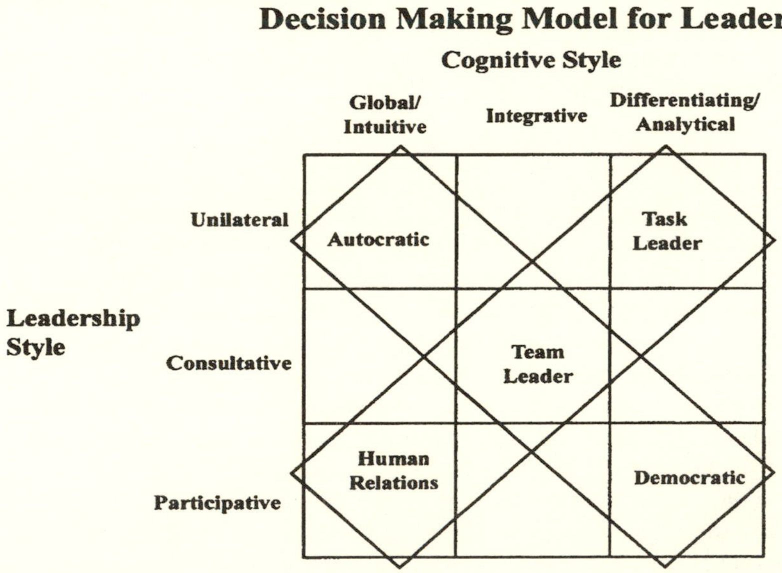

Decision Making Model for Leaders

Cognitive Style

2. Fred E. Fiedler and Victor H. Vroom have worked out elaborate theories on management style and decision making as a function of situational variables. There are many such theories generally grouped under the rubric "contingency theory." The reader is also referred to the following: Paul Hersey and Kenneth H. Blanchard, *Management of Organizational Behavior*, 5th ed. (Englewood Cliffs, N.J.: Prentice-Hall, 1988).

3. Gary Dessler, *Organizational Theory: Integrating Structure and Behavior* (Englewood Cliffs, N.J.: Prentice-Hall, 1980), 17.

4. Duane P. Schultz, *Psychology and Industry*, 2d ed. (New York: Macmillan Publishing Co.,1978), 9–10.

5. Douglas McGregor, *The Human Side of Enterprise* (New York: McGraw-Hill Book, 1960).

6. Ibid., 33–34.

7. Ibid., 47–48.

8. David McClelland, *The Achieving Society* (New York: Free Press, 1967).

9. Frederick Herzberg, *Work and the Nature of Man* (New York: World Publishing, 1966).

10. Amitai Etzioni, *Complex Organizations* (New York: Holt, Rinehart and Winston, 1961).

11. Edgar H. Schein, *Organizational Psychology*, 3d. ed. (Englewood Cliffs, N.J.: Prentice Hall, 1980), 44–45.

12. Bernard M. Bass, "Does the Transactional-Transformational Leadership Paradigm Transcend Organizational and National Boundaries?" *American Psychologist* 52 (February 1997), 130–139.

13. Ibid., 134.

14. Ibid., 133.

15. Ibid., 133.

16. Ibid., 133.

17. Larry Hirschhorn, *Reworking Authority: Leading and Following in the Post-Modern Organization* (Cambridge, Mass.: MIT Press, 1997), 119.

18. Ibid., 27.

19. Richard F. Kankus and Robert P. Cavalier, "Combating Organizationally Induced Helplessness," *Quality Progress* (December 1995), 89–90.

20. Judith R. Gordon, *Organizational Behavior, A Diagnostic Approach*, 6th ed., (Upper Saddle River, N.J.: Prentice-Hall, 1999), 243.

Epilogue: White Coats and Robots

The first round of lectures in Introductory Psychology usually have something to do with psychology as a science. This serves to introduce the idea of scientific method, and the fact that psychology is a science because it does indeed employ the scientific method. Science, after all, is defined not by its subject matter but by method. Psychology, as the science of human behavior, is as much a science as physics is a science since both physics and psychology employ the scientific method. I say this and cognitively I believe it, because it is true. Yet somehow I'm not emotionally convinced, and even as I say the words, I wonder if I really believe what I am saying—that psychology is as much a science as physics because it employs the scientific method. And I cannot help but wonder if the students really buy it either. I talk myself into believing it each year, and I try to talk my students into believing it, but somewhere lurking in the background a question still remains. The issues of objectivity, reliability, validity, control, and most especially, prediction—those things that science is really all about—somehow are different in the social sciences, and my personal case of cognitive dissonance lingers on. Even on exam papers, students rarely handle the question well. There is often reference to physiology or behaviorism or measurement, but an out-and-out statement that psychology is a science because it employs the scientific method is rare. Perhaps it is my fault—perhaps the point has not been made well enough. Perhaps the student can sense my own problem with it so that it does not "ring true," or perhaps the point needs remaking.

Since the first psychological laboratories were established in Europe and in this country in the latter half of the nineteenth century, psychologists have been busy establishing themselves as "true" scientists. Gustav Fechner, Ernst Weber, and Wilhelm Wundt were scientists interested in the problem of psychology. They were primarily interested in bridging the gap that Descartes so firmly established between mind and body. Fechner discounted Descarte's dualism in favor of what has been called the "identity hypothesis," and attempted to reconcile the difficulty by understanding mind as "related to the body as the inside of a circle is related to the outside."[1] Inspired by Weber's early work, he succeeded in formulating what is known today as Weber's law, which holds that there is a constant ratio between a change in the magnitude of the stimulus and a change in the intensity of the perceived experience—that a change in the physical stimulus produces a predictable change in the psychological awareness of that stimulus. The law is with us today, pretty much in the same fashion as Weber first conceived it and as it was elaborated by Fechner. A law? Well, not quite a law, since it was later found that "this ratio does not hold at the extremes, and that in general it is only approximately true."[2]

Ever since Hermann von Helmholtz formulated the law of the conservation of energy, many social and behavioral scientists have been trying to do the same thing, but have succeeded only in approximating, never possessing, the law. Wundt attempted to simulate the physical sciences in his laboratory. William James showed a modest attempt to do so, but never really believed in it, and so gave his laboratory over to a German psychologist by the name of Hugo Münsterberg, who never made much of the Harvard Laboratory. Freud based his psychoanalytical theory on Helmholtzian theory by postulating libido, or psychic energy, which was used variably by the id, ego, and superego—energy used to satisfy eros but finally expended in thanatos—and death came when the energy supply was completely depleted.

The law of the conservation of energy is so mighty in the history of science that it has been looked at longingly by social scientists as something they wish they could make their own, and there has been a relentless search for an equal verity. There must indeed be some kind of organizing principle, some *law of human motion*, if you will, which is the ultimate human principle and which, once discovered, will become the universal paradigm of the social and behavioral sciences. If one accepts the view of Thomas Kuhn, psychology is a pre-paradigmatic science, which has not yet achieved a universal paradigm that all psychologists can use and accept.[3] Of course this is true, if you see as one of the roles of science the establishment of a universal paradigm, one that is useful in all situations. Certainly Kuhn's argument is valid if we admit that a chance meeting of three or more psychologists could very well result in three very different viewpoints of human nature. At worst we are multi-paradigmatic, at best we are pre-paradigmatic. The latter is an optimism that all of our sweat and hard work truly deserves—that is, if we remain intent on discovering that elusive universal paradigm. Some say B. F. Skinner has found it in his principle of operant conditioning, but there are simply too many psychologists who cannot accept conditioning as a universal paradigm.

A conversation I had with my son Billy, when he was 4 years old, has helped to clarify the problem for me. "Daddy," he said, "are you a real doctor?"

"No, Billy, Daddy's not a real doctor."

"Are you a professor?"

"Yes, Billy, I'm a professor."

"But you're not really a professor."

"Why Billy, why isn't Daddy a real professor?"

"Because you don't wear a white coat and make robots."

A child's view of the scientist as provided by the movies and TV is pre-cisely that—someone in a white coat making robots—but this is not unlike the way many adults view science, or indeed how many scholars view science. The white coat is mandatory in this narrow conception of the scientist, who is some-how discovering or harnessing the hidden forces of nature. The scientist is al-ways at the frontier of knowledge. For the scientist, knowledge is its own re-ward. "Philosophy" has a Greek root, but the word "science" has a Latin root. The Greeks enjoyed wondering about things, whereas the Romans were doers, and so the scientist is a doer, he makes "scientia"; he creates knowledge; he dons his "white coat" and goes to the task. "What task?" we may ask. What indeed is the ultimate task of science? The discovery of truth? Poets and artists are somehow equal to that task, I think. Providing valid information about the world? Yes, but a good observer can do that—a good lawyer or good teacher can do that very well. What, then, is the special role of science? I submit that its specialness lies in the question of reliability. Knowledge may be valid, but it must be reliably known so that it can be used with confidence. For this reason, the scientific method is of the utmost consequence. Our measurement instru-ments must be valid and reliable. I can assure you that the social and behavioral scientists have been as scrupulous in this regard as the physical scientists, but for the social scientist, it is a much more difficult task.

Measurement in the social sciences is normative and relativistic, and so it is imperative that experiments be designed in such a way that the experiment can be repeated elsewhere, at another time and place by a different experimenter. The question of *replication* is essential to the scientific method, because it is by replication that we achieve reliability. Reliable knowledge when gained scien-tifically through objective measurement may be the only way such knowledge can be achieved. "Scientia" then, is not just knowledge, it is reliable knowl-edge—knowledge of which we have some measure of *certainty*. The factor of reliability is intrinsic to this certainty. We are certain of knowledge that has been reliably gained.

Recently, a student reported on an article that included the term *soft science* in its title. It is interesting, I believe, that in the literature, we still find a distinc-tion made between *soft* and *hard* science. But I see this distinction not in the sense of social versus physical, intangible versus tangible, inexact versus exact, but rather in the degree of certainty achievable. In the social sciences, certainty is "softer" than in the hard sciences because reliability is so much harder to achieve. After all, the variability the social scientist must contend with is con-tinually changing. The confounding law of individual differences holds true both biologically and culturally so that although all people may share the same human nature, *each* person is different. Variability contributed by cultures, by societies, by organizations, by groups, and by individuals is the kind of variability social science must deal with. That we have come as far as we have is truly remarkable. Thus far there has been no universal model for all cultures (although all human cultures, like ant cultures, hold many attributes in common) nor should we try to invent one—as the "scientist in the white coat making robots" would like to do. I do not believe that social science will ever achieve the universal paradigm of the physical sciences, nor should it try to. Nor are we "fifty years behind" the physical sciences. We are simply very different. We have different problems of measurement, different forms of reliability, and hence different degrees of certainty. I believe it is wrong to refer to the social sciences as pre-paradigmatic. We are multi-paradigmatic and probably even more so *now* than fifty years ago. There was a time when we spoke of five schools of thought in psychology, but we can't afford that luxury any longer. As we learn more, we must necessarily invent new models to deal with the increasing complexity of the problem. We now have behavioral models, cognitive models, psychoanalytical models, interpersonal models, existential models, phenomenological models, and the list goes on. There is indeed a proliferation rather than an amalgamation of topics and courses. There are courses on Child Psychology and the Psychology of Dying and every imaginable topic in between. This is as it should be, and to expect that we can achieve any kind of universal paradigm is foolhardy. To the contrary, we must begin to appreciate and fully understand that we are multi-paradigmatic and what this suggests in terms of interdisciplinary approaches to research and applied social science. Organizational behavior is a case in point, since it pulls from management theory, psychological theory, sociological theory, anthropological theory, and political theory almost equally, and this makes the topic very exciting indeed.

Nor in research will it ever be possible to exercise nearly the kinds of controls possible in the physical sciences. We labor hard to do so, and we appreciate the importance in doing so, but to control *all* intervening variation is just impossible to do. For social science, uncertainty *is* real world, and that's why we build so many logical constructs and so many theoretical models to help us contend with this amount of variability. For social scientists, people are both the subject *and* object of investigation, and this has enormous implications for *objectivity, measurement, control,* and *prediction.* The social sciences are in a very different ball game from the physical sciences—a game that has different rules and different procedures, games in which multiple models operate. In fact, the social scientist plays not one, but many games, and many models are employed.

One might argue that it is a shame that the social sciences have not achieved greater certitude about human nature and human conduct, that there must be a great sense of frustration and futility in being a social scientist. If we are intent on searching for some sort of universal paradigm, then I would agree that it is an inherently frustrating and futile endeavor. On the other hand, if we understand what social science inherently is, futility vanishes. Social science is the science of the indeterminate. It is a science that helps us appreciate and deal with ambiguity—not in the sense of making the ambiguous unambiguous, although it is wonderful when it can do that, but more so in providing us with the logical constructs and the instruments to deal effectively with an ambiguous situation and achieve an intellectual posture that can handle the "maybes" and the "sometimes"—the uncertainties, ambiguities, and vagaries that are, in fact, the human condition.

In very many instances, social science is as much a matter of faith as of certitude, as much a matter of hope as of control and prediction. The psychotherapist *believes* that a certain course of action with a person, based on her reading of psychological research, will be beneficial, and she *hopes* that the patient will improve. The teacher likewise has *faith* that a certain method also based on psychological studies will work, and after trying his best, he *hopes* that achievement will result. The industrial psychologist *believes* that the management development program she helped install based on applied research will enhance management effectiveness, and she *hopes* that performance and productivity will increase in positive directions.

Social science claims that if one can establish a sense of trust in others, groundwork is established for mutual disclosure, acceptance, understanding, and growth—that personality change can occur through the human process of empathy. But consider the amount of variability in this statement regarding empathy. Empathy is tough enough to define, much less observe. How does one observe empathy? How does one measure it? Yet it can be experienced. Consider also the degrees of feeling inherent in the term. How empathic? With whom? Under what kinds of circumstances? That we are able to formulate conclusions from such variability speaks very highly for the progress social and behavioral sciences has made.

I believe that as the world decreases in size, as communications become more rapid, as technology assumes more roles that used to require human ingenuity, the social and behavioral sciences will achieve greater *significance and importance* in helping people develop greater trust in their own reasoning and judgment. To help people assert their values; to provide skills in understanding and helping others, and by providing greater assurance and faith in ourselves, these sciences can help us deal effectively and meaningfully with an enormously complex and uncertain world.

NOTES

1. Robert I. Watson Sr., *The Great Psychologists,* 4th ed. (New York: J. B. Lippincott, 1978), 241.

2. Ibid., 245.

3. Thomas S. Kuhn, *The Structure of Scientific Revolutions*, 2 nd ed., enl. (Chicago: University of Chicago Press, 1970), 178.

Appendix: A Model for Integrating People and Data in Organization Decision Making

This Appendix is a summary of a presentation made by the author at a conference on Understanding Managerial Excellence(see page 117) and is based on research conducted by The Conference Board in which he was a principal investigator.[1] We interviewed the senior management teams of seven major corporations including six chief executive officers. They included two health care manufacturing organizations, two heavy industry manufacturing organizations, a major airline, a major newspaper publishing firm, and a refinery producing petroleum products.

Our research design focused on seven high-level policy decisions made by each organization. We reasoned that a useful way of understanding how managers use information would be to investigate how information is channeled into each decision event. The decisions, therefore, were true-to-life examples of information utilization. In a few cases the company also cooperated in supplying a great deal of factual data including survey results, minutes of meetings and other research documents.

While we began our research in an attempt to assess the cognitive processes involved in decision making, very early in our interviewing it became apparent that the social dimension was equally, if not more important, to consider. This led to the design of the model incorporating both dimensions. See Figure 3 on page 132.

Each interview was conducted by the author and another researcher. Two members of The Conference Board staff assisted from the outset. We worked together in identifying companies, making contact, building a research design and constructing an interview guide. Each interview lasted an hour or more, and since all interviews were taped, this resulted in hundreds of pages of transcribed information. It fell to the author to do the analysis of all information provided by the transcriptions as well as the documentation.

An analytical report was prepared for each decision that included both strategy and process, although the effort was made to focus primarily on information processing. Clearly the Decision Making Model for Leaders (Figure 3) was very useful for this purpose, since each decision could be located within the model. The model is based on the interactive relationship between cognitive style and leadership style. It is not the first time such an interactive relationship was considered, however. In 1970 Terence Mitchell found a positive relationship between cognitive complexity and interpersonal orientation.[2] Later Ferdinand Gul examined the interaction between personality variables and cognition.[3]

In order to account for the interactive effect of both variables a matrix was designed with leadership style as one coordinate and cognitive style as the other. This takes the form of a 3 x 3 matrix as shown in Figure 3. The leadership dimension is described as unilateral, consultative and participative and the cognitive dimension as global-intuitive, integrative and differentiating-analytical. Both dimensions have been independently researched for many years and different styles have been identified along both dimensions that contribute to this 3 x 3 design.

The model provides a framework for understanding how managers use information in the decision making process, moreover the interactive nature of the model adds some new territory to our understanding of information processing in organizations.

The interactive nature of the model produces nine different descriptions of how managers work with data and the ideas of others (see Figure 4, on page 141). We have observed these behaviors in the past, and now we have this tool for understanding social psychological factors that account for these behaviors. According to this model managers with varying cognitive and leadership styles behave in different ways when processing information. For example, two managers who prefer a participative leadership style may behave very differently because their cognitive styles vary.

While all managers in the study contributed variably to decision content, decision ownership was with the chief executive in most cases. In Figure 5 (see page 142), we see the location of each decision within the model.

While we can draw no definite conclusions based on our limited sample, certain tentative observations are suggested. We notice, for example, that decisions tend to cluster toward the center of the matrix, however only two decisions have been identified as team decisions based on collaborative effort. Note also that only one decision out of seven can be clearly shown to be participative, this despite all that is said in recent years about the merits of participative decision making. In fact, true participative decision making was hardly practiced at all. To be sure, group discussion occurs but it is participation in decision content,

Figure 4

Behavioral Descriptions within the
Decision Making Model for Leaders

Cognitive Style

		Global/Intuitive	Integrative	Differentiating/Analytical
Leadership Style	Unilateral	Asserts own views with minimal use of objective data or ideas of others. Relies heavily on one's dominant ideas and values in assessing a problem situation.	Tries to integrate personal values and beliefs with objectively achieved facts. Seeks a "balanced" solution which incorporates both subjective and objective assessments.	Sees need to personally assess all facets of a problem. Sticks to objective data in achieving a "rational" solution. Tries to disallow personal bias.
	Consultative	Seeks opinions of trusted associates. Selectively takes their ideas into account in moderating one's own views. Guided by others, but does not surrender personal assessment.	Sees problem solving as a team effort in which personal views and views of others are openly confronted and discussed but may ultimately resort to one's own best ideas.	Sees the need to confer frequently with others in validating one's own ideas. Inclined to follow lead of others in achieving personal resolutions.
	Participative	Very interested in how others "feel" about a problem. Emphasis is on disclosure and openness. There is optimal sharing and smoothing of feelings in achieving consensus.	There is a deliberate (sometimes time consuming) effort to achieve highly integrative solutions in which feelings and ideas are balanced and worked through. Optimal group solutions are sought and accepted.	Personal prerogatives yield to group process. Primary role is to facilitate optimal sharing and idea processing. There is trust in the capacity of the group to work through and achieve sound solutions which are then implemented.

not ownership, which is revealed in this study. It is one thing to seek input from others, to be an effective listener and be able to process group ideas; it is quite another to move the ownership of the decision to the group. While people appreciate the opportunity to give their opinions on a problem, it is far different to experience the ownership of the decision itself. There is likely a correspondence between a sense of ownership and a sense of commitment. We probably more easily accept a decision we participated in, but are likely to experience commitment to decisions we own. Apparently different CEOs mean different things when they refer to themselves as participative leaders. More often than not their approach is consultative in which they maintain and protect decision ownership. Indeed, in two of the seven decisions researched, the decisions were closer to unilateral decisions than to consultative ones. That decisions gravitate toward collaboration is probably true, but personal control of the decision process is clearly evidenced in these results.

Figure 5

CEO Placement within the
Decision Making Model for Leaders

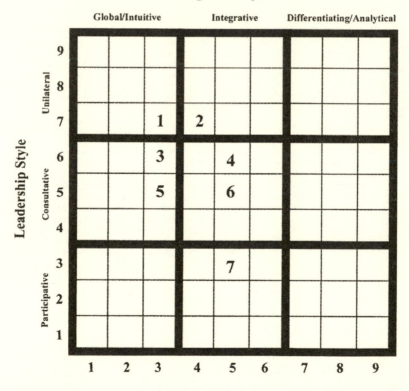

Also interesting to observe is that information searching and objective data analysis contributed only partially and in some cases hardly at all to the decisions in question. Senior level decisions are clearly more experiential and value-based than would be distilled from an objective assessment of facts and opinions. There is only partial scanning of the environment. Decisions seem to flow out of "accumulated wisdom." They represent the assumptions, beliefs and values which were probably used by the same executives in achieving their respective levels of corporate prominence. At this point in the evolution of American management this appears to be the acceptable and necessary style.

It will be interesting to observe what will occur as organizations begin to experience a cultural shift from authoritarian to participative values. Two organizations in our study appeared to be at a point of transition, in which there was a relatively strong team leader characterized by daring and vision. The literature refers to such leaders as transformational, in the sense that they have the capacity to transform the cultures of the organizations they lead. This involves a great deal of attention to social information processing. These are cultures in which a sense of quality and excellence become a reality and there is a feeling of excitement and commitment to the ideals of the organization. Ultimately as a revised culture unfolds and as new norms and values are internalized participative decision making can be more fully experienced. This invariably contributes to decision quality itself. We have observed one such organization in our study.

It is expected that the future will find a more enlightened acceptance of principles drawn from social and behavioral science. That leaders will see that decision quality in terms of values for society and for the organization is enhanced through social information processing. Perhaps decision events now seen in the upper left quadrant of the model will move to the lower right quadrant. Only through the sensitive use of organizational members can this be accomplished.

NOTES

1. This study was conducted in 1984–85. The author thanks David A. Weeks, Senior Vice-President for Research and Program at The Conference Board, who invited the author to initiate this investigation as a sabbatical research project.

The Conference Board is a management information network whose purpose is to help senior business executives and other leaders throughout the world in understanding critical issues on management practice, public policy and economics. This is done through its publications, meetings and conferences as well as information released regularly through the news media.

2. Terence R. Mitchell, "Leader Complexity and Leadership Style," *Journal of Personality and Social Psychology* 16 (September 1970), 166–174.

3. Ferdinand A. Gul, "The Joint and Moderating Role of Personality and Cognitive Style on Decision Making," *The Accounting Review*, 59 (April 1984), 264–277.

Selected Bibliography

Alexander, Richard D., *The Biology of Moral Systems* (Hawthorne, N.Y.: Aldine de Gruyter, 1987).

Allport, Gordon W., *Personality: A Psychological Interpretation* (New York: Henry Holt and Co., 1937).

————.*Becoming: Basic Considerations for a Psychology of Personality* (New Haven: Yale University Press, 1955).

————."The Open System in Personality Theory," *Journal of Abnormal and Social Psychology* 61 (1960).

————.*Pattern and Growth in Personality* (New York: Holt, Rinehart and Winston, 1961).

————."Gordon W. Allport," in, *A History of Psychology in Autobiography*, vol. 5, edited by Edwin G. Boring and Gardner Lindzey (New York: Appleton-Century-Crofts, 1967).

Allport, Gordon W., Vernon, Phillip E., and Lindzey, Gardner, *Study of Values: A Scale for Measuring Dominant Interest in Personality* (New York: Houghton-Mifflin, 1970).

Anastasi, Anne, *Psychological Testing* (New York: Macmillan Publishing Co., 1982).

Baars, Bernard J., *In the Theater of Consciousness* (New York: Oxford University Press, 1997).

Bandura, Albert, "The Self System in Reciprocal Determinism," *American Psychologist* 33 (1978).

Bandura, Albert, Ross, Dorothea, and Ross, Sheila A. "Imitation of Film-Mediated Aggressive Models," *Journal of Abnormal and Social Psychology* 66 (1963).

Bass, Bernard M., "Does the Transactional-Transformational Leadership Paradigm Transcend Organizational and National Boundaries?" *American Psychologist* 52 (February 1997).

Berdyaev, Nicolas, *The Meaning of the Creative Act* (New York: Collier Books, 1962).

Bettelheim, Bruno, *The Informed Heart* (New York: Avon Books, 1960).

Boehm, Christopher, "Some Problems with Altruism in Search for Moral Universals," *Behavioral Science* 24 (January 1979).

Brandt, Lewis W. "Don't Sweep the Ethical Problems under the Rug! Totalitarian Versus Equalitarian Ethics," *Canadian Psychological Review* 19 (1978).

Brown, Norman J. O., *Life Against Death, The Psychoanalytical Meaning of History* (New York: Random House, 1959).

Cavalier, Robert, "Freud's Civilization and Its Discontents," Dana Lecture Series, Elmira College, March 1989.

Cavalier Robert, and Wesp, Richard, "The Garbage-Can Illusion as a Teaching Demonstration," *Teaching of Psychology* 24 (1997).

————."The Perception of Familiar Objects," paper presented at the conference, *Teaching of Psychology: Ideas and Innovations*, Ellenville, N.Y., 23 March 1995.

Cavalier, Robert P., Isenberg, Daniel J., Sternberg, Robert, and Streufert, Siegried, "Understanding Managerial Excellence," presentation given at the Conference Board in New York City, 6 May 1986.

Csikszentmihalyi, Mihaly, *Flow: The Psychology of Optimal Experience* (New York: Harper & Row, 1990).

Dawkins, Richard, *The Selfish Gene* (New York: Oxford University Press, 1976).

Dessler, Gary, *Organizational Theory: Integrating Structure and Behavior* (Englewood Cliffs, NJ: Prentice-Hall, 1980).

Durant, Will, *The Story of Philosophy* (New York: Time Incorporated, 1962).

Emerson, Ralph Waldo, *The Selected Writings of Ralph Waldo Emerson*, edited by Brooks Atkinson (New York: The Modern Library, 1992).

Erikson, Erik H., *Childhood and Society* (New York: W.W. Norton and Co., 1963).

————.*Insight and Responsibility* (New York: W.W. Norton & Co., 1964).

Etzioni, Amitai, *Complex Organizations* (New York: Holt, Rinehart and Winston, 1961).

Fodor, Jerry A., *The Modularity of Mind: An Essay on Faculty Psychology* (Cambridge, Mass.: MIT Press, 1983).

Fox, Ronald E., and Sammons, Morgan T., "A History of Prescription Privileges," *American Psychological Association Monitor* 29 (September 1998).

Frankl, Viktor E., *Man's Search for Meaning* (New York: Washington Square Press, 1984).

Freud, Sigmund, *Basic Writings of Sigmund Freud* (New York: Modern Library, 1938).

————.*Civilization and Its Discontents*, translated and edited by James Strachey (New York: W. W. Norton & Co., 1961).

————."Outline of Psychoanalysis," quoted in Ernest R. Hilgard, *Psychology in America* (New York: Harcourt Brace Jovanovich, 1987).

Friedman, Meyer, and Rosenman, Ray H., "The Key Cause—Type A Behavior Pattern," in Sources: *Notable Selections in Psychology*, ed., Terry F. Pettijohn (Guilford, Conn.: Dushkin Publishing Group, 1994).

Gay, Peter, *The Freud Reader* (New York: W. W. Norton & Co., 1989).

Goleman, Daniel, *Emotional Intelligence* (New York: Bantam Books, 1995).

Gordon, Judith R., *Organizational Behavior: A Diagnostic Approach*, 6th ed., (Upper Saddle River, NJ: Prentice-Hall, 1999).

Gul, Ferdinand A., "The Joint and Moderating Role of Personality and Cognitive Style on Decision Making," *The Accounting Review*, 59 (April 1984), 264–277.

Harlow, Harry F., "The Nature of Love," *American Psychologist* 13 (1958).

Harré, Rom, *Social Being: A Theory for Social Psychology*, (Oxford: Basil Blackwell, 1979).

Hergenhahn, B. R., *An Introduction to the History of Psychology* (Pacific Grove, Calif.: Brooks/Cole, 1997).

Hersey, Paul, and Blanchard, Kenneth H., *Management of Organizational Behavior*, 5th ed. (Englewood Cliffs, N. J.: Prentice-Hall, 1988).

Herzberg, Frederick, *Work and the Nature of Man* (New York: World Publishing, 1966).

Higgins, E. T., and Sorrentino, R. M., eds., *Handbook of Motivation and Cognition*, vol. #2 (New York: Guilford Press, 1990).

Hillman, James, *A Blue Fire*, edited by Thomas Moore (New York: Harper and Row, 1989).

Hirschhorn, Larry, *Reworking Authority: Leading and Following in the Post-Modern Organization* (Cambridge, Mass.: MIT Press, 1997).

Hofstadter, D. R., *Godel, Escher, Bach: An Eternal Golden Braid* (New York: Vintage Books, 1980).

Holland, John L., *Making Vocational Choices* (Englewood Cliffs, N.J.: Prentice-Hall, 1973).

————.*Professional Manual for the Self-Directed Search*, 1979 edition (Palo Alto, Calif.: Consulting Psychologists Press, 1979).

Huxley, Aldous, "Education on the Non-Verbal Level," in *The Healthy Personality*, edited by Hung-Min Chian and Abraham H. Maslow (New York: D. Van Nostrand, 1977).

James, William, *The Principles of Psychology*, 2 vols. (New York: Dover, 1890/1950).

————.*Psychology: The Briefer Course* (New York: Harper Torchbooks, 1892/1961).

Janis, Irving L., *Victims of Groupthink* (Boston: Houghton Mifflin, 1972).

Janis, Irving, and Mann, Leon, *Decision Making* (New York: Free Press, 1977).

Jung, Carl, *The Portable Jung*, edited by Joseph Campbell, translated by R. F. C. Hull (New York: Viking Press, 1976).

Kankus, Richard F., and Cavalier, Robert P., "Combating Organizationally
    Induced Helplessness," *Quality Progress* (December 1995).
Kant, Immanuel, "Prolegomena to Any Future Metaphysics," quoted in Morton
    Wagman, *The Sciences of Cognition* (Westport, Conn.: Praeger, 1995).
————.*Critique of Pure Reason*, translated by N. K. Smith (New York: St.
    Martin's Press, 1965).
Kast, Fremont E., and Rosenzweig, James E., *Organizations and Management:
    A Systems Approach* (New York: McGraw Hill, 1974).
Krutch, Joseph W., *The Measure of Man* (New York: Bobbs-Merrill, 1954),
    quoted in Gordon W. Allport, *Becoming.*
LaPiere, Richard, *The Freudian Ethic* (New York: Duell, Sloan and Pearch,
    1959).
Lewin, Kurt, "Collected Writings," in *Field Theory in Social Science: Selected
    Theoretical Papers*, edited by D. Cartwright (New York: Harper, 1951).
Maier, Norman R. F., *Problem Solving and Creativity in Individuals and
    Groups* (Belmont, Calif: Wadsworth, 1970).
Maslow, Abraham H., "A Theory of Human Motivation," *Psychological Review.*
    50 (1943).
————.*The Farther Reaches of Human Nature* (New York: Penguin Books,
    1982).
————.*Toward a Psychology of Being* (Princeton: Van Nostrand, 1962).
May, Rollo, *Love and Will* (New York: Dell, 1969).
————."Freedom, Determinisim and the Future," *Psychology*, trial issue (April,
    1977).
May, Rollo, ed. *Existential Psychology* (New York: Random House, 1961).
McAdams, Dan P., *The Person: An Introduction to Personality Psychology*
    (New York: Harcourt Brace, 1994).
McClelland, David, *The Achieving Society* (New York: Free Press, 1967).
————.*Human Motivation* (Glenview, Ill.: Scott, Foresman and Co., 1985).
McGregor, Douglas, *The Human Side of Enterprise* (New York: McGraw-Hill
    Book, 1960).
Milgram, Stanley, "Some Conditions of Obedience and Disobedience to
    Authority," *Human Relations* 18 (1965).
Miller, Arthur G., *The Obedience Experiments* (New York: Praeger, 1986).
Mitchell, Charles E., *Individualism and Its Discontents: Appropriations of
    Emerson, 1880–1950* (Amherst, Mass.: University of Massachusetts Press,
    1997).
Mitchell, Terence R., "Leader Complexity and Leadership Style," *Journal of
    Personality and Social Psychology* 16 (September 1970), 166–174.
Morris, Charles, *Varieties of Human Value* (Chicago: University of Chicago
    Press, 1956).
Murray, Bridget, "Data Smog: Newest Culprit in Brain Drain," *American
    Psychological Association Monitor* (March 1998).
————."Weave Your Own Web Site: An Essential Tool, Resource," *American
    Psychological Association Monitor* (March 1998).

Murray, Edward J., "Possibilities and Promises of Eclecticism," in *Handbook of Eclectic Psychotherapy*, edited by John C. Norcross (NewYork: Brunner/Magel, 1986).

Nagel, Thomas, "What Is It Like to Be a Bat?" in *Readings in Philosophy of Psychology*, vol. 1, edited by Ned Block (Cambridge, Mass.: Harvard University Press, 1980).

Newman, Fred, and Holzman, Lois, *The End of Knowing: A New Developmental Way of Learning* (New York: Routledge, 1997).

Pascal, Blaise, *Pensées*, trans. by A.J. Krailsheimer (London: Penguin Books, 1966).

Patterson, Cecil H., and Watkins Jr., C. Edward, *Theories of Psychotherapy* (New York: Harper Collins College Publishers, 1996).

Rogers, Carl, *On Becoming a Person* (Boston: Houghton Mifflin, 1961).

Rogers, Carl R., *Toward a Modern Approach to Values: The Valuing Process in the Mature Person*, in *Reading in Values Clarification*, edited by Howard Kirschenbaum and Sidney B. Simon (Minneapolis: Winston Press, 1973).

Rosenbaum, Ron, *Explaining Hitler: The Search for the Origins of His Evil* (New York: Random House, 1998).

Rychlak, Joseph, *Artificial Intelligence and Human Reason* (New York: Columbia University Press, 1991).

Sagan, Carl, *The Dragons of Eden* (New York: Ballantine Books, 1977).

———.*The Demon-Haunted World* (New York: Ballantine Books, 1996).

Sartre, Jean Paul, *Existentialism and Human Emotions* (New York: Philosophical Library, 1957).

Schein, Edgar H., *Organizational Psychology*, 3d ed. (Englewood Cliffs, N. J.: Prentice Hall, 1980).

Schneider, Kirk J., "Toward a Science of the Heart," *American Psychologist* 53 (March 1998).

Schultz, Duane, *Growth Psychology: Models of the Healthy Personality* (New York: D. Van Nostrand, 1977).

Schultz, Duane P., *Psychology and Industry*, 2d ed. (New York: Macmillan Publishing Co., 1978).

Schweitzer, Albert, "I Resolve to Become a Jungle Doctor," in *The Healthy Personality*, edited by Hung-Min Chian and Abraham Maslow (New York: D. Van Nostrand, 1977).

Seligman, Martin E. P., "Depression," in *Sources: Notable Selections in Psychology*, edited by Terry F. Pettijohn (Guilford, Conn.: Dushkin Publishing Group, 1994).

Sheldon, William H., *The Varieties of Temperament: A Psychology of Constitutional Differences* (New York: Harper and Brother, 1942).

Simon, Herbert A., *Administrative Behavior: A Study of Decision-Making Processes in Administrative Organizations*, 2d. ed., (NewYork: Macmillan Publishing Co., 1957).

Skinner, B. F., *About Behaviorism* (New York: Alfred A. Knopf, 1974).

Skinner, B. F., *Beyond Freedom and Dignity* (New York: Alfred A. Knopf, 1976).

Spranger, Eduard, *Types of Men*, translated by Paul J.W. Pigors (Halle: Max
    Niemeyer Verlag, 1928; New York: Hafner Publishing Co.).
Sternberg, Robert J., *Introduction to Psychology* (New York: Harcourt Brace
    College Publishers, 1997).
Szasz, Thomas S., *Ideology and Insanity: Essays on the Psychiatric
    Dehumanization of Man* (Garden City, N. Y.: Doubleday, 1970).
Thorndike, Edward L., *Animal Intelligence* (New York: Macmillan Publishing
    Co., 1911).
Tolman, Edward Chace, *Principles of Purposive Behavior* in *Psychology: A
    Study of a Science,* vol. 2, edited by S. Koch (New York: McGraw Hill,
    1959) in B. R. Hergenhahn, *An Introduction to the History of Psychology*
    (Pacific Grove, Calif.: Brooks/Cole Publishing, 1997).
Tucker, Robert C., ed. *The Marx-Engels Reader* (New York: W. W. Norton &
Co.,   1978).
Von Bertalanffy, L., *Organismic Psychology and Systems Theory* (Worcester
    Mass.: Clark University Press, 1968).
Wagman, Morton, *The Sciences of Cognition* (Westport, Conn.: Praeger, 1995).
Watson, John B., *Behaviorism* (New York: W. W. Norton & Co., 1925).
Watson, Robert I., Sr., *The Great Psychologists,* 4th ed. (New York: J. B.
    Lippincott, 1978).
Wilson, Edward O., *On Human Nature* (Cambridge: Harvard University Press,
    1978).
Winter, David G., *Personality, Analysis and Interpretation of Lives* (New York:
    McGraw-Hill, 1996).
Wolman, Benjamin B., ed. "The Historical Roots of Contemporary Psychology,"
    quoted in B. R. Hergenhahn, *An Introduction to the History of Psychology*
    (Pacific Grove, Calif.: Brooks/Cole, 1997).
Woodworth, Robert S., *Dynamics of Behavior* (New York: Henry Holt and Co.,
    1958).

Index

About the Author

ROBERT P. CAVALIER is Dana Professor of Psychology at Elmira College. He is a counseling and organizational psychologist with interests in human motivation and organizational behavior. Before joining the Elmira College faculty he was Director of Education and Training for the American Institute of Banking of the American Bankers Association. He was associated with the Laboratory of Psychological Studies at Stevens Institute of Technology as a counseling and industrial psychologist and was Director of Educational and Vocational Counseling at Fairleigh Dickinson University. He has done research and consulting for several major corporations and professional organizations including the American Hospital Association, Compeer, the National Center for Manufacturing Sciences, and The Conference Board.

ISBN 0-275-96168-0

EAN

9 780275 961688

HARDCOVER BAR CODE